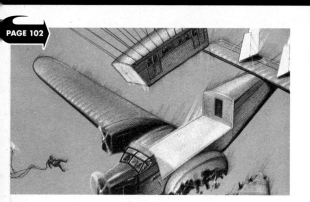

PAGE 102

1932 **FACING DOWN DISASTER** The transport airplane of the future will feature a giant parachute for the detachable cabin.

PAGE 117

1931 **LAUNCHED VIA CATAPULT** The seaplane of the future features folding wings and launches from a submarine.

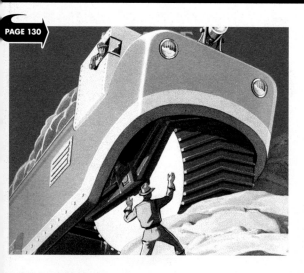

PAGE 130

1940 **AMPHIBIAN TANK** Adaptable over ground, water, and mud, this tank will carry troops into battle.

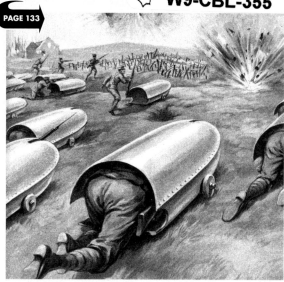

PAGE 133

1915 **STEEL PUSH CARS** This wheeled body shield is the latest scheme developed for protecting infantryman during offensive operations against enemy trenches.

PAGE 180

1958 **TO THE VACUUM OF SPACE** This fantastic rocket-propulsion system will propel and control future satellites in orbit.

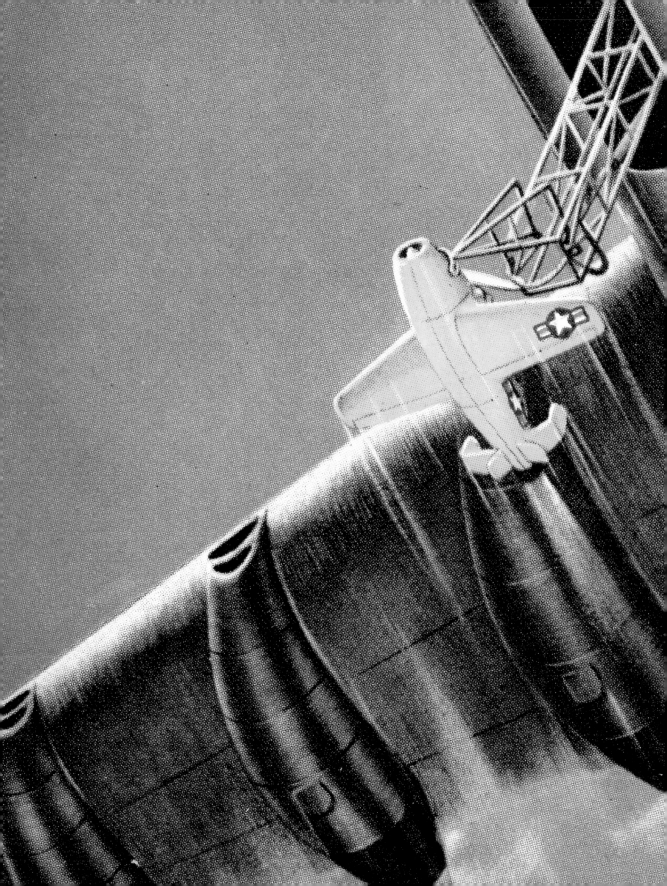

THE AMAZING
WEAPONS
THAT **NEVER** WERE

ROBOTS, FLYING TANKS & OTHER MACHINES OF WAR

GREGORY BENFORD
and THE EDITORS of
Popular Mechanics

HEARST BOOKS
New York

CONTENTS

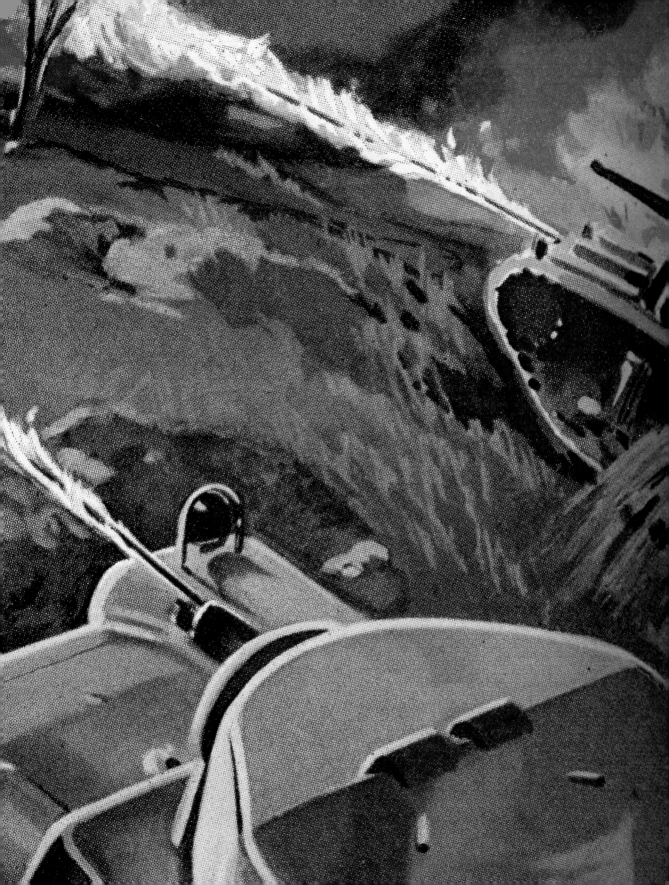

FOREWORD

Popular Mechanics magazine opened in 1902, a few months before the Wright brothers launched their first successful flight and well before both World Wars. It was almost impossible for our editors and writers back then to imagine what weapons might be found on the battlefield in 2012, but that didn't stop them from trying. Since then, we've published countless predictions of engineers, scientists, and inventors as steam gave way to electricity, horses were overtaken by tanks, and advances in transportation and telecommunications seemed to shrink the world.

Now we live in an era we're used to thinking of as "the future." Though we still lack flying tanks and death rays (as predicted in 1932 and 1925), our missiles are guided by computers (as we forecast in 1947), our submarines are powered by nuclear reactors (1958), and our government uses spy satellites (although perhaps not in the way we anticipated in 1958—see page 142). Surrounded by wonders and a fast-evolving culture of innovation, it's just as challenging today for us to imagine the next century as it must have been for our early 20th century colleagues to envision the fabled year 2000.

So we decided it was high time to take a look back at the predictions of the past, not only to score them for accuracy (some are shockingly prescient, some hilariously wrong) but also to pay tribute to the inventiveness of the past. We hope this collection of articles and essays, which first appeared in *Popular Mechanics* between 1903 and 1969, will instruct as well as help recall the awe felt by previous generations of readers when they heard about the first steamless battleship, sat down at the first "teaching computer," and saw the airplane take its place in the arena of war. Join us on a trip to yesteryear and discover the many amazing weapons of tomorrow.

The Editors of *Popular Mechanics*

INTRODUCTION

BY GREGORY BENFORD

THE DREAM OF VIOLENCE
Why we fight, and why we're smart about it

> *"Science fiction is to technology as romance novels are to marriage: a form of propaganda."*
> —JASON PONTIN, editor of MIT's *Technology Review*

War is a human constant. The Old Testament runs rife with conflict, cities burned black and populations slaughtered as the streets run red. Archeologists know that warfare started as soon as we had towns, and probably even before that. Consult today's newspaper for updates, quite similar to the times when there were fewer than a million of us—10,000 years ago.

But then, war isn't our invention. Surely the primates coming before us did it; their burials show a lot of injury. Better evidence lies in chimpanzees, who separated from us genetically six million years ago, and do carry out warfare between troops of a few dozen. Apparently they are driven by need for territory and competition for food.

But though chimps are very strong, they mostly just corner their opponents and beat them to death. They don't pick up a club to get better leverage in a brawl, as in the opening sequence of *2001: A Space Odyssey*. Insects also don't use weapons in their famously ferocious wars; these are basically huge unarmed combats that do follow battle plans, but tools seem beyond them.

Using weapons is uniquely human. We carry out sustained war, and for that you need technology. That image in *2001: A Space Odyssey* shows a hominid throwing his first tool—a weapon—into the air in celebration of newfound abilities. The bone tumbling in air turns into an orbiting weapons platform millions of years later.

Weapons are the essence of human warfare. At first, more was better. But as we've learned in the Long Peace after 1945 (when nation state warfare casualties dropped an order of magnitude), quality trumps quantity. In our time, the use or threat of lethal force to break the will of the enemy often works precisely because our weapons are so terrible. The best weapon of all is one that never needs to be used.

In 1832, Carl von Clausewitz famously referred to war as the "continuation of political intercourse, carried on with other means." In the 20th Century, those means

were mostly technologies. The diplomatic maxim here is "Speak softly and carry a big stick." All that's changed in our history is the stick itself.

FUTURE VISIONS

A single factor determined most 20th century wars: Failure to foresee the full influence of science and technology on weapons and engineering.

Ignoring the positive effect of railway and motor transport on mobility led the Russians to defeat in World War I. Not applying the common radio to combat units destroyed the French Army in 1940. Neglecting the menace of the submarine, and delaying development of countermeasures, nearly lost Britain World War II. The Japanese overcame a major Western power in 1905, by mastering battleship armor and tactics better than complacent Imperial Russia, which assumed an Asian power could not use modern weaponry effectively and so did not keep its armaments and strategy up to date.

Every major power in World War II had a nuclear weapons program, though, prompted by their own nuclear scientists. It was stream engine time—the tech emerged forcefully from the science. (Leo Szilárd was first; the idea of critical mass in a uranium warhead came to him in 1933, while he crossed the street shortly after reading an H.G. Wells science fiction novel, *The World Set Free,* about "atomic bombs.") It was the big new possibility, developed less than a decade after the theoretical idea arose. The Japanese erased records of their nuclear program after Hiroshima and Nagasaki, but before the Allies landed in Tokyo. They wanted to maintain that *they* hadn't thought of such a destructive weapon.

The first half of the 20th century was a slaughterhouse, and the second half a relative golden age. One invention made that happen: Nuclear weapons, used twice and so far, never again. Their power, well displayed in over a thousand tests in the USA alone, frightened the world. Large state warfare ceased. But not the invention and deployment of new weapons, often cited as necessary to "keep the peace" by intimidation and by arming for worse-case scenarios.

Though we see small conflicts spattered across our news, these are comparatively peaceful times—brought, ironically, by the deadly efficiency of our weapons. Historically, eras of peace arise when men of war have influence, not when politicians dominate. Caesar's legions enforced the Pax Romana. The 19th century Pax Britannica came not from crafty diplomats but from the Royal Navy and His Majesty's Forces. We dwell in a similar era.

We live in the first age benefitting from weapons so terrifying we cannot use

them. *Popular Mechanics* magazine may have unwittingly advanced the cause of this peace by its attention to the dazzling weaponry it lovingly reported. Here we revisit the magazine's visions, to see how they stack up against what we now know of warfare and the infernal but fascinating devices it spawns.

ULTIMATE WEAPONS

War isn't our invention, as a species, but in modern times, quite clearly invention fuels the outcomes of wars.

In the pulp science fiction magazines of the 1930s, predictions of the "ultimate weapon" that would end all wars were common. *Tech triumphant!* Harry Truman was a terrific reader of pulp adventure stories while in the U.S. Senate. This made him comfortable with the sudden revelation that the "atomic bomb" existed, on the day President Roosevelt died (April 12, 1945). Truman knew that the United States fire bombing of Tokyo in spring of 1945 had already killed nearly a hundred thousand. The American public was in no mood to stall.

Clausewitz had emphasized the inherent superiority of defensive measures suggests that habitual aggressors are then likely to wind up failures. In early 1945, most military figures thought this was still true, despite the success of the Blitzkrieg (which Russian tactics stopped in 1943). All

that was to change in a striking reversal of the defense/offense advantage.

Truman's situation harked back to the Doolittle Raid on Tokyo in 1942, which caused little damage but had important ramifications. The attack raised morale in the United States and made a hero out of its commander, Lieutenant Colonel James Doolittle. He had triumphed because he saw that bombers taking off from aircraft carriers could spring a surprise over distances the Japanese thought impossible. Nobody had even thought of the bomber idea. The shock of this new technology altered the entire war, not because of the minor damage, but because of human reactions.

Japan's weak air defenses embarrassed the Japanese military leadership. They moved four fighter groups from the Pacific to defend the home islands. Mostly these sat around, defending the emperor, while the crucial turn in the war occurred far away.

To prevent further attacks, the Imperial Japanese Navy launched an offensive in the Pacific Ocean that ended in defeat. They too considered the raid deeply embarrassing, and attempted to close the perceived gap in their Pacific defense perimeter. This led directly to the decisive American victory at the Battle of Midway in June 1942, when the Japanese ventured near Hawaii, looking for a knockout blow, not knowing that meanwhile the Americans had cracked their secret code and knew where their fleet was going.

In an attempt to retaliate against the Doolittle Raid, the Japanese also began developing a new technology: fire balloons capable of carrying incendiary and anti-personnel bombs from Japan to the continental USA—another innovation that worked. The USA kept news of the devastating fires out of newspapers. The Japanese intelligence network, which had some access to U.S. newspapers, assumed the balloons were not getting through—and the high command stopped the program. Here the best weapon was cleverness.

Still, the ultimate weapon beckoned. The first firebombing of Tokyo on the night of March 9–10, 1945, was the single most destructive air attack of the war, and seemed the peak of destruction. That night 279 bombers dropped 1,665 tons of bombs, causing a massive firestorm that overwhelmed Tokyo's civil defenses and destroyed 16 square miles—seven percent of the city's urban area. 83,793 people were killed and 40,918 injured, and over a million lost their homes. Terrible weapons indeed.

Neither of the bombs which fell on Hiroshima or Nagasaki killed as many, but they had enormously psychological effect because the bombs were totally new.

The horror of two bombs doing so much is the essence of our modern strategy of nuclear Mutual Assured Destruction, appropriately abbreviated MAD. Supporters of the bombings emphasize the strategic significance of the targets. Hiroshima housed the headquarters of the Fifth Division and the 2nd General Army, commanding the defense of southern Japan with 40,000 military personnel in the city, most at ground zero of the bomb. Hiroshima was a communication center, an assembly area for troops, a storage point and had several military factories as well. The second bomb target, Nagasaki, had wide-ranging industries making ordnance, ships, military equipment, and other war materials.

A counterpoint to arguments against the nuclear bombs is that area bombing, though horrible, had been accepted and used by every major belligerent in the war for the past six years: Britain, France, Germany, the United States, Italy, Japan, China and the Soviet Union had all used large-scale area bombing. Indeed, the largest such was the March 1945 Tokyo raid. If such bombing did not reach the same scale as Hiroshima or Nagasaki, it is only because of technical limitations rather than a lack of will or desire. In fact the Axis powers invented this tactic, only to see it used and improved upon by the Allies. Both world wars showed that horrors silence humanitarian objections, in the desire to get it over with.

In this, the psychology of terrible weapons has many fathers.

HARD MACHINES, SOFT MEN

"...a man is only a fragile bag of skin filled with obscene mysteries...(or) your own body betrays you with a wounding, and you feel the moment of shattering pain and then the seductive, helpless numbness of shock."

—JOE HALDEMAN, Vietnam veteran and author

War technology allows us to not think so directly about the tender beings who guide them. Troops meet on the battlefield not only the murdering enemy, but the surprisingly easy killer that lurks within.

Unsurprisingly, the United States as the first democratic military power moved quickly to minimize casualties through technology. Citizen armies don't like to see bloodied ranks. The American style of warfare has stressed trading munitions for lives. We shot from behind concealment in the Revolutionary War, and fought many telling battles against the British at sea, because our ships were lighter, quicker and could maneuver well against big battleships. Over the long term the United States used lots of artillery, even to find out what the enemy was doing—"reconn by fire" instead of sending out patrols.

My father fought in World War II and told me of interrogating German officers who were amazed at how much ordinance—artillery, bazookas, bombs—we would throw at even a few infantry and tanks. This became a signature of the democracies, where losses had political impact: Lessen human casualties through better weapons. Make the enemy pay the human cost. When you do have losses, send them home in antiseptic plastic bags.

Better still, let the machines do your fighting: Invent robots.

Popular Mechanics foretold the role of robots in combat, and these ideas are now bearing fruit. Robot warriors, drone aircraft, semi-autonomous "tanks" with machine guns—these now operate in the Middle East. They all first appeared in science fiction and then in *Popular Mechanics*.

Robots are war's newest wrinkle, new and deadly. Not only do young men get a rite of passage, a chance to show their valor, and perhaps channel frustrations and aggressions—they get to do it with toys.

Technology also primes the economic pump. The United States came to dominate the aircraft industry after World War II, and has only lately given much ground. Research and development of the 747 and other aircraft came from defense innovations first introduced in long distance hauler aircraft like the C-147, in fighter planes, and many other battlefield stalwarts.

Still, the atom bomb led many to think, *Maybe we ought to cut this stuff out before we get ourselves killed.* The American response was a rash of civilians building bomb shelters. The Swiss went further, building shelters for their entire population. Fear helped the cause of large-scale peace.

Though one might title this book *Wonderful Mechanisms for the Wholesale Killing of Humanity,* war's purpose is not death. As I learned early in officer training, nations use war to impose their will on enemies.

For example, during the Clinton administration Serbian air war in 1998, the United States lost no pilots in battle. All casualties were Serbian, and they folded within a month—the first such clean, one-sided defeat by air power in history. Air war had come into its own at last, nearly a century after *Popular Mechanics* saw it coming.

Reflecting on these enormous events, in our present time we can learn useful lessons for the 21st Century. We know the past but cannot influence it; we can influence the future but cannot know it.

Terrible weapons have frightened us, but they have led to an uneasy peace. Few saw this coming in the 1940s, when many wise men predicted nuclear war within a decade or two. Instead, now minor wars fester but do not lead to large-scale conflicts like those from 1914 to 1945.

No general peace seems plausible, in the decades ahead. In a way, looking back can show ourselves in our most brilliant and boneheaded moments, and both are illuminating. If we remember the perspectives this book can yield, we may make our way through turbulent times. ◎

In the 20th Century, imagination took flight, from H.G. Wells to the Jetsons. We saw impossible airplanes and super-weapons galore. These prophecies of the past help to demonstrate the power of the American imagination on the canvas of the future. The slaughterhouse of the first half of that century meant that many of these visions were about weapons. In a world beset by fascist and communist dictators, having better weaponry seemed not only a good idea, but often an essential one.

Popular Mechanics was an avid fan of tech-heavy ideas, like 1942's super-speed bullets, which inevitably failed practical tests. A chamber that contains higher pressures weighs more, so the resulting rifle is harder to lug through rice paddies. Faster bullets blow through your target and do less damage, too.

Instead, the United States used the reliable M1 in World War II, but this did not work well in muddy, wet terrain. However it could be unjammed and even fixed in the field. (In the Army Reserves I once learned to take apart and reassemble, blindfolded, the classic M1 of the World War II vintage. In the Vietnam fields, that skill became nearly impossible.) Optimized performance in one situation may be terrible in another.

War spawned many pessimistic predictions, like those made in 1921's "Chemicals to Replace Guns in Wars of Future." As late as 1931, *Popular Mechanics* still thought that, while "at all peace conventions, the diplomats decry the use of gas in future warfare, everybody in position to know about these matters realizes that gas will undoubtedly be employed in the next war."

Thankfully, they were wrong. Gas had done so much damage to troops in World War I trenches that the Geneva Convention's 1929 ruling stuck. Mustard gas led to invention of the first gas masks (although the most-used and low-tech defense of unprotected troops was to wrap their heads in urine-soaked gauze). To the surprise of many, while many nations have stockpiled chemical weapons, only a handful have ever used them since the end of World War I.

In 1945, *Popular Mechanics* accurately foresaw fully industrialized warfare, as well as weapons of mass destruction. The realization slowly dawned that Mutually Assured Destruction (MAD, a brilliant acronym), meant the nuclear option of all-out war was no longer survivable. This, however, didn't stop the United States and Soviet Union from their nuclear arms race, until their stockpiles had reached the point that they could ensure the destruction of the entire planet. Eventually, both sides primarily shifted to developing conventional arms for limited wars.

At the height of the cold war, nukes were everywhere. In a 1961 article, *Popular Mechanics* enthused: "GIs are getting

Sled dogs have been used successfully to haul both cannons and search and rescue teams during the Great War.

PREDICTION
1914

SUPER-SPEED BULLETS KNOCK 'EM DEAD

PREDICTION 1942 **The ordinary .22 rifle will hardly knock down a rabbit.** But its new big brother has been used in every part of the world against all sorts of big game—and every animal it has hit has dropped dead in its tracks.

It may sound like a futuristic ray gun comic strip, but it's real. The tiny .22 pellet, weighing about one-tenth of an ounce, travels at super-high velocity and kills by hydrostatic shock. It has the same effective range as an army rifle but has a drop of only 4.25 inches at 400 yards—compared with the four-foot drop of service ammunition. It explodes on contact even with a twig, yet it is armor-piercing.

The bullet's terrific speed does the trick. The pellet gets its tremendous velo-city from an oversize powder charge that would blow the gun to pieces if it were not for the carefully shaped of cartridge, which has been designed to direct the expanding gas out through the barrel. The sudden and intense pressure to which a live target is subjected, even when the skin is hardly creased, disorganizes nerve centers all over the body, resulting in immediate death.

There is a rumor that super-high velocities already have been adopted by the Germans for one anti-tank gun design. Barrels for such guns can be replaced at frequent intervals. The special cartridges would be no more of a supply problem than the special shells that are now required. Since an ultra-high-velocity bullet is both armor-piercing and explosive, it does the same job as a high-explosive shell at less cost. (*Continued on page 26.*)

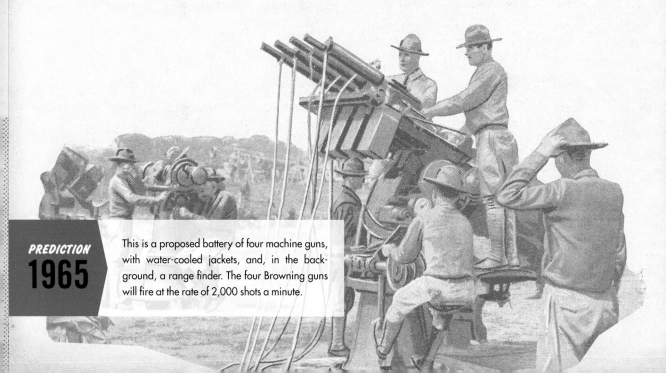

PREDICTION 1965 This is a proposed battery of four machine guns, with water-cooled jackets, and, in the background, a range finder. The four Browning guns will fire at the rate of 2,000 shots a minute.

Stafing enemy planes are a menace to soldiers on the ground. Soon, multiple anti-aircraft guns will be mounted in an armored cupola on the rear of half-trucks to protect our men.

PREDICTION
1943

A long-barreled rifle is awkward to handle in or out of a car and unhandy even when carried in a saddle holster. The new design is much easier to manipulate in close quarters. Gunsmiths therefore think the high-velocity firearm will eventually be adopted for parachute troops, motorized troops, and other groups that must operate in confined spaces.

NOISEMAKER ON GUN *SAVES SOLDIERS' EARS*

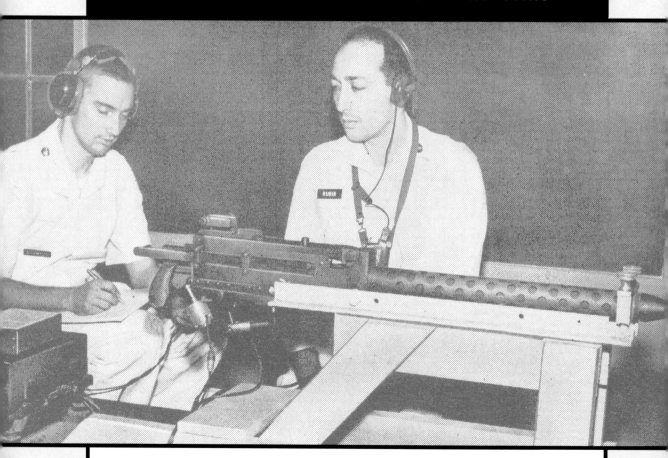

Tests have shown that if a harmless "beep" is sounded one-fifth of a second before a gun is fired, two tiny muscles in the inner ear contract, an automatic protective mechanism that deadens the sound of the weapon. Future weapons will produce a protective noise automatically.

PREDICTION 1947 According to Captain C. V. Gandy of the Arms and Ammunition Division, powerful 57-mm. and 75-mm. recoilless rifles will change the conduct of warfare as much as the invention of gunpowder did, give the all-important infantry the striking force of an artillery unit.

The recoilless rifle was tested briefly in combat toward the end of the war and yielded highly satisfactory results. The shoulder-fired 57 resembles the bazooka in appearance, but is not to be confused with rocket weapons. In the recoilless rifle, only the shell goes through the air. The pack howitzer, the smallest of the 75-mm. artillery pieces, weighs 1,200 pounds; the 75-mm. portable recoilless rifle weighs only 105 pounds. This rifle can be carried into action by four men and fired from terrain inaccessible to conventional artillery.

PREDICTION 1965 The "duplex" rifle cartridge, a new development that significantly increases a soldier's ability to hit his target by firing two bullets simultaneously with each shot, should contribute in a big way to the effectiveness of guerrilla fighters, especially when it is adapted to the smaller hand weapons of the Special Forces. The second bullet, which nestles into a cavity in the base of the first, does not follow exactly behind the first bullet when fired, but deviates slightly to increase the radius of the strike area.

TINY WEAPONS FOR HOT LITTLE WARS

PREDICTION 1962 How can the United States give its Southeast Asian allies more anti-guerilla firepower without weighing them down with heavy guns and ammunition?

For them, the Defense Department is developing radical new weapons and is vastly improving some of the reliable stand-bys of non-nuclear war. One of the newest and most radical—the "micro-jet" rocket— is a hard nylon needlelike projectile about one inch long. Nobody in the Pentagon can confirm details, but the micro-jet is apparently very much like a toy missile sometimes found as premiums in Cracker Jack boxes. But to this "toy" has been added a tiny solid-propellant rocket.

The weapon can be fired accurately from soda-straw size plastic or aluminum tubes for several hundred yards with a speed nearly twice that of a standard .30-caliber military rifle bullet. The almost noiseless projectile will penetrate thick plaster walls and small tree trunks. One fighter can discard his rifle and move lightly with just the small plastic straw and a pocketful of rocket-darts. A number of launching straws can also be grouped together to fire a devastating barrage, still controlled by just one man—an anti-guerilla fighter who will become a running, jumping, hiding, attacking missile battalion.

Rocket motors powerful enough to drive a spaceship to the moon are getting trial runs in a variety of guided missiles.

FUTURE WARS WILL BE WON WITH SUPER-ROCKETS

PREDICTION 1945 The stratosphere rocket, in its present development, cannot be **used against the United States** with enough success to make it worthwhile. But strategists admit that in a future war a super-rocket, carrying really heavy explosives, might not only prove to be the decisive weapon but could conceivably annihilate entire areas of civilization as well.

PREDICTION 1947 No one has yet successfully guided a supersonic missile, except for a **few test models of a German flak rocket.** (Because the guidance of a German V-2 functions only when the rocket is burning, it is therefore actually "guided" much as an artillery shell is aimed.) Despite the many factors to be overcome in perfecting guided missiles, Colonel Simon says: "It is reasonable to expect that long-range rockets and guided missiles will largely replace the tactical and long-range bombing planes, the long-range gun, and the large antiaircraft gun."

PREDICTION 1948 Acoustic air fuses will be tested in the anechoic room of the magnetism research program at White Oak. The acoustic air fuse is a new type of weapon with great possibilities. The Nazis began experiments with it during the war.

NAZI LAND TORPEDOES
THREATEN RUSSIAN TANKS

Using torpedoes as land weapons is a military innovation claimed by the Germans. This anti-tank land torpedo used by the Nazis in Russia is about the size of a motorcycle sidecar and carries about 150 pounds of explosive in its nose. A reel of cable leads 1,500 yards to an operator in a shelter, who guides the machine and sets off the explosive by means of electricity. The best Russian defense has been to cut the cable.

German fighter planes would fly above an American air formation and drop "air mines" equipped with acoustically sensitive fuses. The mines exploded when they fell within sound range of the American-made motors.

"In the next war—which we hope will never come—there can be no delaying action," pointed out Admiral Beatty. "We hope to have completed a large backlog of pure and applied research that can be translated immediately into weapons. There won't be any time for research in a world of atomic weapons, proximity fuses, and supersonic guided missiles."

CHEMICALS TO REPLACE GUNS IN WARS OF FUTURE

PREDICTION 1921 **Canned, solidified poison gas, claimed to be absolutely foolproof and mobile, has been perfected for use by** the American soldier, according to Brigadier General A. A. Fries, head of the Chemical Warfare Service in Washington. In addition to the development of new forms of gas, army experts at Edgewood have had to improve the gas masks to make them effective against some of the new gases developed there. As a result, the United States now has not only gases that surpass anything used during the World War, but a mask that, in recent tests, was worn 24 hours a day for a week, except at mealtime,

without any discomfort whatever. Breathing was normal, speaking was simple, and it kept out all the gases thus far known.

The operation now is for each man to take from his pack, at the propitious meteorological moment, a package of gas and apply heat: the poisonous vapors roll away on the wings of the wind into the heart of enemy territory. No other agent, except intense heat, can release the gases. A mere handful of officers trained for the work can pick the time for miles of frontline trenches to belch forth destruction.

PREDICTION 1931 **At all peace conventions, the diplomats decry the use of gas in future warfare,** but all who know about these matters realize that gas will undoubtedly be employed in the next war. Some experts even assert that the next war will be fought nearly entirely with gas.

One recent developments is the use of a gas that will seep under a mask and cause sneezing or vomiting, forcing the soldier to remove his mask in the presence of other gas that then strangles or paralyzes.

PREDICTION 1936 **The next war will likely begin in an immeasurably terrible manner.** There will be no warning. Some gray morning there will be ear-splitting explosions, so frequent as to sound like a steady roar. The confused and terror-stricken inhabitants of a city will rush in panic to windows to see buildings exploding and falling into the

The soldier of the future will be equipped with oil tank, goggles, and mask, ready to attack with burning oil.

PREDICTION
1915

streets. Fires by the thousands will break out; streets will be choked with maddened men, women and children struggling through the wreckage; bursting water mains will flood the streets: gas mains will belch fire and death-dealing gas; electric service wires will writhe and flash. Chaos such as civilization has never beheld will reign supreme.

With the city aflame, deadly poison gas will rain down from the skies and send to death the last remaining inhabitants. After a few of these surprise attacks, the nations will settle down to the business of destroying one another. Then those wonderful mechanisms for the wholesale killing of humanity and the destruction of property that science and engineering have developed in recent years will be disclosed.

It has been proposed to make use of deadly diseases that Europeans and Americans have never encountered and to which, in consequence, they are very susceptible. It is reasonable to believe there are stored away in the secret chambers of several war departments thousands of gallons of disease cultures ready for distribution.

PREDICTION 1936 Thinking men are asking themselves what the next war will be like. The World War was the most terrible event civilized man has ever witnessed. If another breaks out, and nations take advantage of all the amazing developments which science and engineering have made available since 1918, what are the consequences likely to be? Among other preparations, this German soldier is training a war dog to be equipped with a gas mask to go through gas fumes.

MAKING HUMANE WAR WITH ANESTHETIC GAS

A thousand airplanes, each carrying 5,000 pounds of chloroform, could put the inhabitants of cities as large as Chicago or New York to sleep in a few moments—and, similarly, planes flying above trenches might induce peaceful slumber in whole battalions of soldiers. They could be awakened later having suffered relatively little harm.

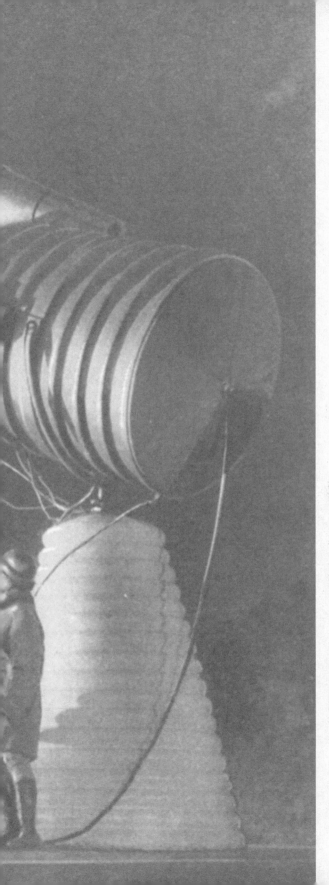

THE WEIRD WHISPERS OF DEATH

PREDICTION 1925 **Said to be more destructive than any previous invention of its kind,** a new death ray discovered by a German scientist has an effective ground range of 40 miles and operates to an altitude of more than 45,000 feet. Men and animals are rendered unconscious by the mysterious force of its waves, whose paralyzing influence lasts for six hours, according to reports to the Department of Commerce.

PREDICTION 1928

VIBRATING QUARTZ PRODUCES *DEADLY SOUND WAVES*

Alfred L. Loomis has discovered that this quartz crystal apparatus, producing vibrations at the rate of 2.5 million per second, can slaughter small organisms in water. Plant and animal cells were killed by the violent stirring of their contents, although the cell walls of the plants were not broken, as they were evidently too tough and strong.

POWER *from*

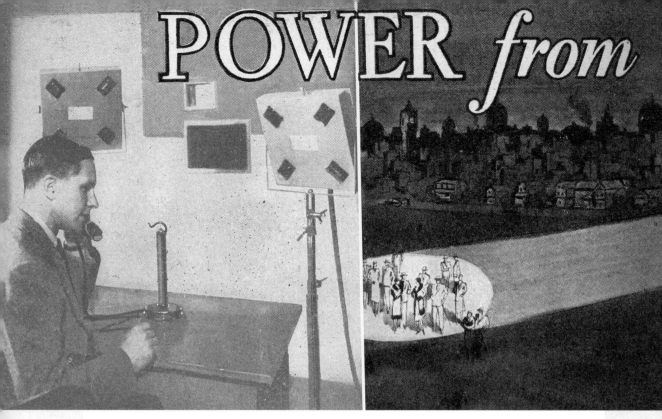

PREDICTION 1933 The invisible infrared rays from the spectrum of sunshine are predicted to be used in the future for dispersing fog in railroad operations, in anti-fog lighthouses and warning buoys around coasts, aboard liners and freight steamers, for speeding up transport by sea and land, and as landing lamps on airdromes. Life rays also suggest death rays, and lethal rays of the kind are known to have been used by certain air departments in the European war.

While scientists are not agreed as to the power of the so-called death ray, the men who operate the heavily charged mechanism take no chances on being injured by backfire from the tremendous current. They wear special rubber suits to insulate themselves from the apparatus. The base of the gun, a beehive-shaped affair that revolves, is composed of porcelain and rubber, while the coils in the three hornlike projections on the barrel are so arranged that the heat they emit will not harm the rest of the machine.

PREDICTION 1927 Sound waves so far above the audible pitch that no ear can detect them may drive submarines from the ocean in the next war. Professor Robert W. Wood of Johns Hopkins University, the inventor, declares that all living matter—plant or animal—will perish if placed in the path of his ray.

The death sound, however, is restricted in its passage to two mediums—solid and liquid—and cannot be transmitted through the air. But as it will pass readily through water and then through the solid hull of a

the INVISIBLE World

PREDICTION
1945 Without warning, the ground trembles as if from a local earthquake and a roaring blast afflicts eardrums. The improbable stratosphere rocket had paid a visit. This new manifestation of indiscriminate warfare, known as V-2s, is actually less destructive than its predecessor, the V-1, the "buzz bomb" with wings.

AT THIS POINT SPEED REDUCED TO ABOUT 2,000 M.P.H.

MILES

Stratosphere path of V-2 which trav

submarine, its development may prevent the submersible from ever again being a threat to peace.

The audible range of the average ear covers a band of from 16 to about 15,000 cycles. Dr. Wood uses vibrations of 350,000 to 400,000 cycles per second. With them he has killed fish in tanks of water, mice and other small animals, as well as plants.

Development of a "death ray" was one of the problems tackled by inventors during the war, and though several have since claimed success, none of their efforts proved fully successful when tried by experts. The latest report is of a new ray produced in France, for which complete success is claimed; it was tested recently in the engineers' barracks at Montpelier before French army officers.

Blast area of V-1 (above) is greater

PREDICTION
1933 **Recent discoveries by scientists in American and European laboratories** suggest that man's coming control of cosmic forces will dim all that science has done in the past century and a half.

Sir James Jeans, well-known British astronomer and physicist, says, on the other hand, that these cosmic rays are

EARTH TREMORS

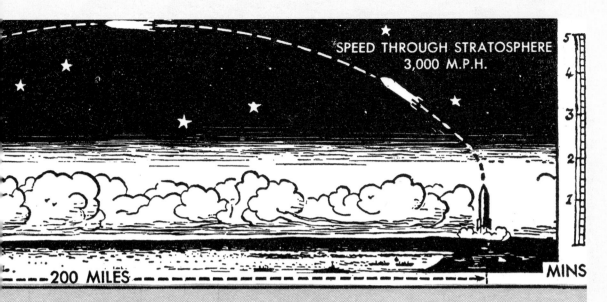

SPEED THROUGH STRATOSPHERE
3,000 M.P.H.

5
4
3
2
1

MINS

←---- 200 MILES ----→

200 miles in about four minutes. At takeoff it weighs 13½ tons

AREA OF BLAST

EXPLOSION

COMPLETE
DEMOLITION

n the V-2 (below) which digs deep crater when rocket explodes

AREA OF BLAST

EXPLOSION

CRATER

breaking down millions of atoms in us, every second of our lives. "They may be essential to life, or they may be killing us," he adds.

Life rays also suggest the other side of the picture—death rays—and lethal rays are known to have been used by certain air departments in the European war, when they were employed to stop, suddenly and unaccountably, hostile airplanes in transit across frontiers to bomb cities. The full story of their use in the war has yet to he revealed.

PREDICTION 1936 A recent discovery is the lethal quality of ultra-high frequency, high-amplitude sound waves. Transmitted into water, they kill every living thing—even the smallest bacteria. Directed at persons, they create violent nausea and a long list of disabilities, some of which are fatal. Directed at large structures of light weight, such as airplane wings and propellers, they create vibrations violent enough to wreck the structure. By altering the frequency to suit the natural period of vibration of a given object, they will actually "fiddle the bridge down," so to speak. Just what has been accomplished in adopting this principle to warfare is not known.

PREDICTION 1938 War may become a battle of sounds, as well as of bullets and bombs. A system for bombarding the ears of the enemy with all the horrible noises of the battlefield has been patented by a French citizen. It consists of playing phonograph record through a loudspeaker network to create a terrific din.

PREDICTION 1960 The death ray, that fantastic invention of science-fiction writers, may someday be a terribly real weapon of both the United States and the USSR. Few scientists are talking about it, but scattered reports indicate that both governments are interested in developing a neutron bomb—a device that could destroy men with bursts of radiation but, like the fictional ray, would leave buildings and machines unharmed.

The subject came to light recently when U.S. Senator Timothy J. Dodd of Connecticut told reporters he has learned that "such a bomb can theoretically be produced by tailoring the energy of a fusion explosion so that, instead of heat and blast, its primary product is a burst of neutrons."

Such a bomb would be a formidable weapon, for it would create little blast damage. A city could be bombed without destroying property. It would produce little uncontrolled fallout, so the bomb could be used without contaminating friendly forces or areas that would have to be entered by troops.

According to Senator Dodd, the bomb would be fashioned from the same ingredients that go into the hydrogen bomb—heavy hydrogen and a little lithium. There has been

talk that TNT or another ordinary explosive could be used to set off a neutron bomb.

PREDICTION 1962 **The army won't admit it's working on a laser weapon,** but spokesmen admit such a weapon is entirely feasible. In one experiment, a scientist focused a medium-power laser beam on a spot 2 millimeters in diameter and burned a hole through ten tempered steel razor blades with one extremely short pulse of light.

Maser-based weapons are also in development; the letters stand for "microwave amplification by stimulated emission of radiation." Masers take radio waves or light waves (in which case they're called optical masers, or lasers), boost them hundreds of times, then shoot them off in a powerful, concentrated beam. The light they generate within the cone is more than a million times brighter than the sun. It is also hot enough to burn a hole through everything from razor blades to people. It could be, in fact, a genuine death ray. Portable versions of it already have been built.

TAMING THE H-BOMB

PREDICTION 1950 **The military implications of the hydrogen bomb lead us far into the unknown.** When we try to anticipate the effects of weapons as powerful as the hydrogen bomb, we must face those possibilities calmly. We must assume that the hydrogen bomb can be made not only by us but by Russia; that it can be made at a not-too-excessive cost, given the economic capabilities of both nations; that it can be delivered to almost any target on the earth's surface; and—if we are to give credence to recent news reports—that it will be as much as 1,000 times as powerful as the A-bomb.

With the development of the hydrogen bomb, even as few as five or six planes would be able to make an extremely damaging attack without warning. Such an attack could not cause us to surrender overnight, but it could greatly prolong the war which would ensue.

Atomic bomb parts could be brought in by enemy agents and assembled in spots most dangerous to us. It might be possible, likewise, for hydrogen bomb parts to be smuggled in and put together. Certainly, the assembled bombs, either atomic or hydrogen, could be secreted into our harbors in enemy merchant ships. Similarly, such bombs, hidden in our cities, could be exploded without warning—or used as leverage in an ultimatum demanding our complete and immediate surrender.

The claim has been made publicly, by certain scientists, that the use of the hydrogen bomb could annihilate all life on this planet, and by others that it could destroy the Earth itself. In making these statements, these men were presumably speaking of extremely remote possibilities, rather than of probabilities. One should not be alarmed by such gloomy prognostications.

Troops watch a nuclear explosion from a safe distance away. In the near future, the threat of an H-bomb could be used to demand surrender.

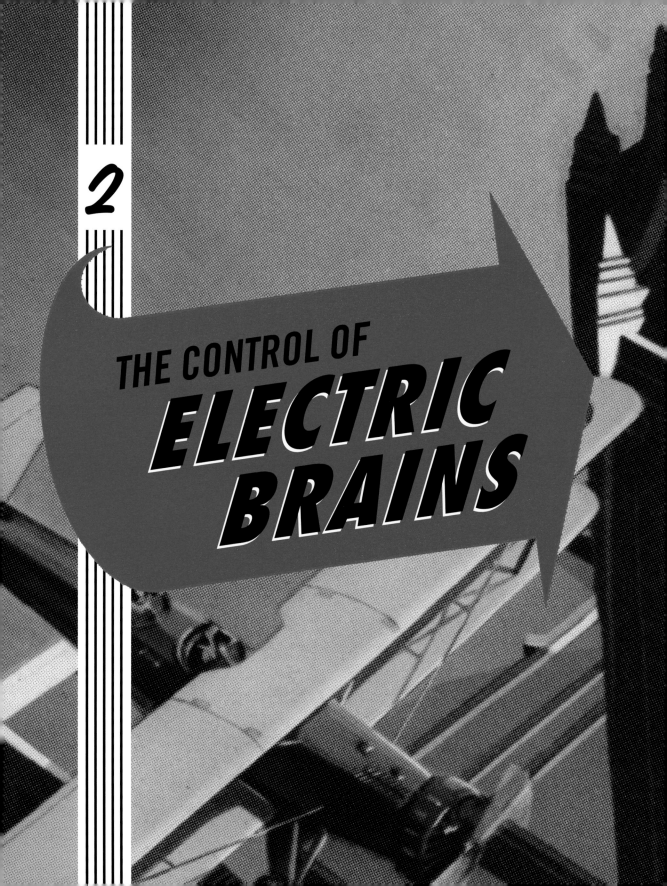

2

THE CONTROL OF ELECTRIC BRAINS

In warfare, rugged often beats smart. Early issues of *Popular Mechanics* foresaw some of the changes to come, but even in World War II, my father, who was an artillery officer at Normandy, found that both American and German gunners did their sighting calculations by hand. Not much was done by computers, because they didn't at first work well in real field conditions.

The technology used in the 1940s was quickly outdated by 1960s tech. Smart guided missiles, infrared heat-seeking sensors, and surface-to-air missiles (SAMs) would radically alter both anti-aircraft and offensive warfare once they were launchable from jets or other aircraft.

Popular Mechanics glimpsed the coming missile age in 1944, noting dryly the problems that an unmanned robot or missile sent over the Atlantic might face, like inaccuracy and the tons of fuel such a weapon would require. Here 'robot' means the self-guiding missiles, like the German V-2, except grown to massive size. Certainly using fuel to deliver explosives was a dicey cost/benefit issue, but the development of nuclear warheads erased that worry completely.

Not everyone liked robots. A 1934 article provoked fears of planes without human pilots. (Interestingly, an article penned in 1945 demonstrated that wartime experience had largely silenced such fears.)

Today, nearly all planes turn over the majority of tasks to computers (not the mechanical couplings of 1934) and pilots can even fall asleep from boredom. In fact, this even led to Korean Air Lines Flight 007 being shot down by Soviet interceptors in 1983. The crew failed to make a simple switch between navigation systems, and the Russian MIG pilot reported all in the cockpit seemed to be asleep when he could not get their attention. (As a direct result, President Ronald Reagan made the United States Army's Global Positioning System (GPS) available for civilian use.)

"There is only one answer to robots, and that is robots," *Popular Mechanics* said in 1934. Robotic tasks abound now. The drone planes of 1950 and the camera-carrying drone of 1957 all prefigured the many drones we have now. These manifest everywhere today: light planes that can be hand-launched by troops for short range recon; overhead Predator drones armed with missiles in Afghanistan, all managed by satellite from Florida; and silent prop planes that can fly for days, tracking people and cars from high altitudes. To avoid civilian casualties, a single operator sitting in a comfortable chair 10,000 miles away can fly a missile through any window she selects in a building—and is able to change her mind in the last ten seconds before impact.

Army photographers capture 36 square miles of terrain in a single snap of their latest aerial mapping cameras.

PREDICTION
1941

WAR UNDER THE SEA

Likewise, "teaching machines" are commonplace in today's military training, from flight simulators for fighter pilots to the "cyber" flight training of commercial pilots. Now even tank crews train in simulators. All these teaching devices have found their way into industry and schools, with computers making the systems far more accessible. "Hands-on" guidance at a distance profits from kids who train on computer games.

Such 1960s ideas of "programmed learning" have spread into Artificial Intelligence systems that now answer phone calls, help people make reservations or check bank balances, and even sift through our genomes, looking for telltale warning signs of future disease. When your bank answers with some smart software about your balance inquiry, few realize it comes from 1957's "set of 'vocal cords' that allows an electronic brain to say what it is 'thinking' in any language." (This must be the first sign of those phone messages that right away ask you to choose a language.)

We see in these stories a general feature. Standing up to the mud, rain, grit, and grunge of the battlefield matters a lot when new weapons venture out. But the "electronic brains" of vacuum tubes evolve into chips the size of postage stamps. In the end, being smarter prevails. ◉

SHELLS THAT FLY ON THEIR OWN POWER

PREDICTION 1928 **Wars of the future will be battles between mechanized wizards,** mute masses of steel energized by electricity, seemingly endowed with almost human intelligence. Mammoth guns with "eyes" that see the enemy many miles away and can hurl huge projectiles with remarkable accuracy farther than the length of a marathon racecourse will add new efficiency to tomorrow's wars.

The primary difficulty in ground defense against aircraft during the war—and indeed until the last few months—was in getting the fire of the high-angle guns anywhere near the target. The practical solution for this problem, a new fire-control instrument for anti-aircraft guns (it hasn't received a compact name as yet), is the sensation of the day among artillery experts.

One widely circulated story declared that the fire-control instrument picks up the sound of the approaching plane and automatically trains the gun on it, without the intervention of any human direction at all. This is a bit too good to be believed, but even the sober facts are remarkable enough. Manned by a few competent operators, the machine really will automatically compute all the firing data necessary for the handling of a battery attacking a target at any range and altitude.

It will be an uncanny sight to see a battery of guns, wholly deserted by their crews, following with their muzzles every movement of a target speeding through the clouds, as if they were alive. This automation places the whole work of training the guns in the hands of the battery commander, and leaves the gun crews nothing to do but shove the noses of their projectiles into the fuse setters for a moment, slam them into the breeches of their pieces, and pull the lanyards. This makes for very rapid and uninterrupted fire.

PREDICTION 1939 **Shells used in anti-aircraft warfare are given "eyes"** by the Bofors ordnance factory in Sweden so they can "see" their target and burst when they approach it. In the nose of the shell is a cartridge of magnesium, which burns brilliantly during flight and sends out long fingers of light through radial openings in the shell casing. If some of these beams strike an airplane they are reflected back to the shell, where they are caught by photocells. These are connected electrically to operate the detonating mechanism. It is not necessary for the shell to make a direct hit to bring down a plane: the concussion and the flying steel splinters are usually enough to destroy it.

New anti-aircraft guns aim themselves automatically, with remarkable accuracy in hitting targets 2 miles away moving through the air at 200 miles per hour.

PREDICTION
1938

Cannon firing shells that will fly by their own power with jet propulsion may be the outgrowth of a gun designed by Edward F. Chandler, a New York engineer. The first experimental weapon is a light metal tube four feet long and three inches in diameter shooting a shell six inches long and a little more than two inches thick. 18-foot-long jets used to drive non-military projectiles supply the basis for the present gun. Power and distance have already been achieved, but the problems of accuracy in flight, economy in construction, and types of fuel have not been solved.

PREDICTION 1944 **In the shape of today's rocket may be seen the shadow of the next and more terrible war,** unless the United Nations is wise enough to prevent that tragedy. Scientists scoff at speculation over giant robots that might be sent across the Atlantic because of the inaccuracy of any long-range robot and the tons of fuel such a weapon would require. However, a huge launching site captured near Cherbourg was believed to have been ready for a monster brother of the winged robot bomb already blitzing London. The launcher might accommodate a rocket bomb carrying five tons of explosives.

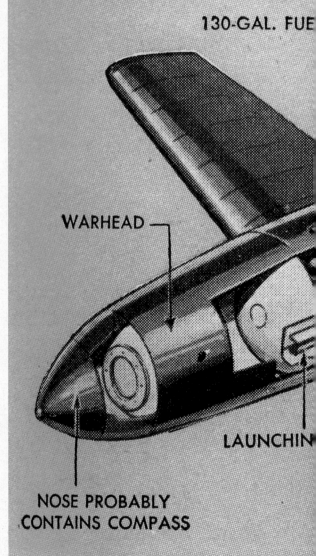

130-GAL. FUE

WARHEAD

LAUNCHIN

NOSE PROBABLY
CONTAINS COMPASS

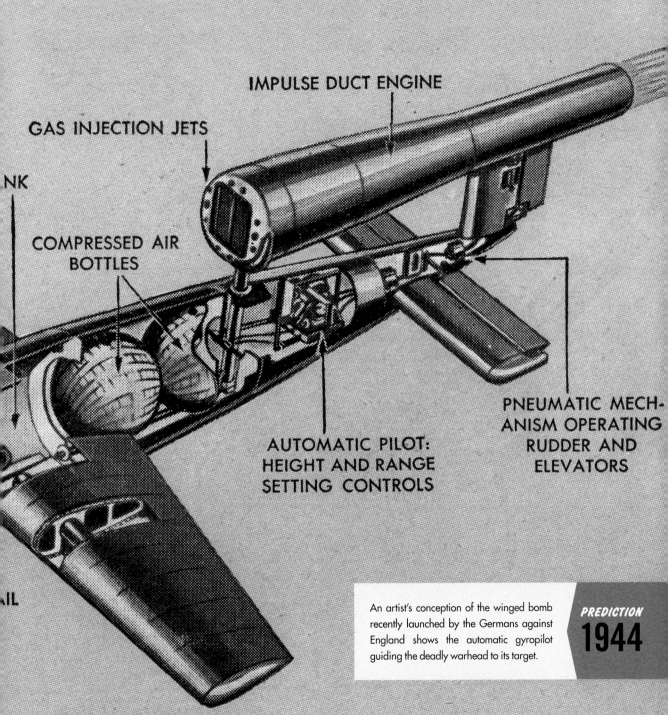

IMPULSE DUCT ENGINE

GAS INJECTION JETS

NK

COMPRESSED AIR
BOTTLES

AUTOMATIC PILOT:
HEIGHT AND RANGE
SETTING CONTROLS

PNEUMATIC MECH-
ANISM OPERATING
RUDDER AND
ELEVATORS

AIL

An artist's conception of the winged bomb recently launched by the Germans against England shows the automatic gyropilot guiding the deadly warhead to its target.

PREDICTION
1944

AIR FORCE TESTS *FLYING "SHARKS"*

These tiger-toothed, fire-engine-red "fish" soaring over New Mexico's sand dunes are Firebee pilotless-jet target drones. After an electric bomb-salvo switch launches them from special racks mounted beneath the wings of a B-26, they are maneuvered by signals from a control box operated by an officer on the ground.

PREDICTION 1947 **National Advisory Committee for Aeronautics scientists recently described the Tiamat rocket as the "first guided missile** to be flown successfully through a predetermined program of maneuvers." Built as a flying guinea pig for future supersonic robot weapons, it is over 14 feet long, weighs more than 600 pounds, and flies faster than 600 miles per hour. Data on its speed, control movements, degrees, and speed of roll are relayed from instruments in the missile to the ground by telemetering.

Among the various guidance systems are the preset mechanisms such as those that steered the German V-1 and V-2 missiles; target-seeking devices such as those that direct the Bat glided bomb on a collision course with its target; the command system by which radio impulses or other signals are used to control the missile during flight; and the course-seeking system by which a beam of light or radio energy is pointed at the target and along which the missile flies until it hits the target. Each of these guidance systems can be used with the same missile.

Smaller missiles that are being studied at Point Mugu include Little Joe, a ship-launched radio-controlled rocket with a two-mile range for use against suicide planes or other missiles, and the radio-controlled Gargoyle for air-to-ground use.

PREDICTION 1954 **Surface-to-air missiles (SAMs) will eventually make up our last line of defense against enemy bombers.** They are anti-aircraft rockets fired from ground launchers and usually arc-propelled into the air by a booster unit that falls away when its power is exhausted. Then the

PREDICTION 1947 An officer checks the antenna that lets ground troops direct this experimental radio-controlled rocket missile.

rocket's own motor takes over and drives it at supersonic speed. These missiles home in on bombers so rapidly that their pilots have no time to take evasive action.

Air-to-air missiles (AAMs) soon may replace the small rockets, now carried by defensive aircraft, that must be aimed to intercept an aerial target. The new missiles do their own aiming once they have left the mother aircraft, and they home in on their targets by means of built-in radar systems.

One of the goals in this new kind of armament is to develop a true intercontinental guided missile. By definition, such a missile would be able to carry a heavy warhead to a selected target as far as 4,000 miles away. Undoubtedly, the only kind of warhead carried by a transoceanic missile would be an atom bomb, because of the tremendous cost involved in the project.

The next step at White Sands will be to refrigerate an entire guided missile in a big, mobile deep-freeze igloo, then immediately place the missile on a launcher and fire it. Eventually, the climatic laboratory will build some enormous chambers in which the biggest rockets can be frozen or heated, undergo atmospheric pressure changes, and be shaken in simulation of flight vibration all at the same time.

PREDICTION 1956 **Rear Admiral J. H. Sides, the navy's guided-missile chief, has this to say** to those who would write off the navy for missilery: "Let me assure you that this would be the mistake of a lifetime! We are accustomed to this specialized environment, and we know how to cope with it."

The gadgetry in some of our missiles would turn Rube Goldberg green with envy. Missiles can do celestial navigation, using star-tracking telescopes that activate "educated" photocells or that can steer by measuring the earth's magnetic currents. Some "smell out" the target by radar, by measuring its heat emission or by sensing its electromagnetic activity. Some even rival CBS—they scan the target and send a TV picture back to the launching point, where the bombardier can watch the screen and guide the missile into the target.

Our streamlined task forces in any future war will have the elusiveness of a bantam and the Sunday punch of a heavyweight. When the bell sounds, chances are they'll already be far at sea, carrying the fight into the enemy's corner and smothering him with blows he never saw coming.

One gnawing worry creeps occasionally into the bull sessions of these missile teams as they pause for coffee—what would happen if the enemy should manage to slide a missile of his own down their radar beam? The practical problems of doing this are well-nigh insuperable, but still.

ROBOT PILOTS TO FLY SHIPS

PREDICTION 1934 **Through the Golden Gate steamed a lean grey destroyer,** no different to the casual eye from any of the sea greyhounds frequently seen traversing that waterway. But on that entire craft there was no human being. Its engines turned, speeded up, and slowed down without the touch of a hand. As deserted as any derelict, it nevertheless performed its every function as though manned by a full crew.

Half a mile behind it was another destroyer—this one fully manned. On its bridge was a metal box about the size of a portable radio. Standing beside this, his hand on a small keyboard, was Lieutenant Commander Boyd R. Alexander, commandant of the navy's mobile target division No. 1 and inventor of the world's

PREDICTION 1927 A radio-controlled submarine, operated from a distant ship, that can wage an attack without risk to our sailors—an American invention that came just too late for use in the Great War.

The robot warship has eerily deserted decks cluttered with radio receiving equipment. Caps over the smokestacks protect them from falling bombs.

first robot fighting ship. From time to time Commander Alexander's fingers depressed a series of the white keys—there are only nine of them altogether—in such combinations as a pianist might use in playing a few chords. Each time the ship ahead changed its course or its speed, or both. Once it tooted twice at a fishing boat.

It is as offensive and defensive units of the navy's active forces that the most important and startling possibilities of the robots are to be realized. Out in those blue wastes where there is still some privacy in a crowded world, the robots have been tested in mock naval engagements of many different varieties. These experiments have revealed some of the incredible things that may be expected of the robots in time of war. The robots have been maneuvered against actual fleets; their guns have been fired upon moving targets.

There is only one answer to robots, and that is more robots. While an enemy would probably never get a chance to copy one of ours—for it would be blown up as he stepped on board—ships based on the same principle will, of necessity, be devised by other nations. It may be a long time before they will hit upon a mechanism that will operate as effectively, but they will assuredly develop some type of ship operated by remote control. And then robot fleets will meet and fight it out in the open sea.

These will be battles in which no lives can be lost, and which the only conscious participants will watch through spyglasses. Imagine the possibilities of maneuvering when neither leader need hesitate, for humanity's sake, to sacrifice a "piece," and when the pieces can be played upon as deftly as the stops of a flute!

PREDICTION 1936 **In the next war, crewless planes loaded with high explosives will be sent out by the hundreds.** These planes are directed by radio. A high-frequency radio beam is emitted, and the crewless ship is adjusted to stay in this beam. The beam can be guided by its emitting station, so the plane can be led around as desired. Its position at every moment is known from radiations either automatically emitted by itself or by reflections of the guiding beam.

Streams of these flying torpedoes directed at a large city, munitions manufacturing center, or supply depot, and arriving and exploding every few minutes, day and night, have the power to deal death and destruction far back of the firing lines.

In the next war, we also face an unmanned airplane attracted by infrared heat radiations. It will follow the nearest plane discharging hot exhaust gases, which emit infrared heat radiations. Small and carrying no load, the ships travel at super speeds and also have the corner-cutting advantage of a pursuer. This unmanned craft will chase an enemy plane, overtake it, and crash into it. It would be difficult to imagine a more uncanny enemy.

PREDICTION 1943 **Super-bombers capable of carrying half-carload lots of bombs bigger than blockbusters** across the Atlantic and back again—without refueling—are promised by General H. H. Arnold, army air forces chief, in *Army Ordnance* magazine. The planes will have "eyes" that will help guide them to their targets or warn of the approach of enemy interceptors, and even plot the course of the pursuers. For defense, they will be armed with cannons even larger than the 37-mm. guns now carried by some fighters. These cannons will be mounted in multiple turrets and operated from a central aiming position comparable to the fire-control system of surface warships. While paying high tribute to the Flying Fortresses and Liberators, General Arnold declares that the new super-bombers will render these craft obsolete.

Plans for the construction of floating islands in the Atlantic to facilitate aviation have been presented. The unique port, as planned, will be 450 yards long, 250 yards wide, and be built at an estimated cost of about $13 million dollars.

PREDICTION
1925

PILOTLESS HELICOPTER IS A SUBMARINE KILLER

Remotely controlled, an unmanned drone helicopter can take off from the deck of a destroyer in any weather, fly to an area where sonar gear has detected an enemy submarine, hover until instructed to drop its homing torpedo, then fly back for rearming—without risking a pilot.

PREDICTION 1947 **Engineers are conducting research on a wide range of pilotless target aircraft.** These small drones have a wingspan of around 10 feet. All are controlled by radio from the ground. They are used as targets by anti-aircraft gunners and also for the testing of new radio control systems for pilotless aircraft or missiles. Some are powered by conventional gasoline engines, some by pulse jets. Some can fly at the rate of 240 miles per hour, climb 25,000 feet, and remain aloft for more than an hour.

Radio control of the drones has been so perfected that a "pilot," standing on the ground, can maneuver one of the craft with as much dexterity as if he actually had his hands on the plane's controls. Holding a small control box from which protrudes a switch handle similar to the control stick of an airplane, the pilot pulls back on the stick to cause the drone to climb or pushes it forward to make the plane dive. Moving the stick left or right swings the plane in the desired direction.

At his command the plane loops, spins, shuttles back and forth only a few feet off the ground, or climbs practically out of sight. He lands the plane by tripping a special switch on the side of the box. This switch sends out the radio impulse that pops open a hatch in the plane's fuselage and frees its parachute, at the same time killing its engine. The plane floats down to a slow landing.

Push-button warfare is still in the future. "We are not yet ready to push the button," remarks Captain A. B. Scoles, director of tests at Point Mugu, "but we are doing everything possible to wire up the button so that if the occasion arises, our buzz will be just as loud and just as effective as the other fellow's."

SHARPER EYES FOR THE FLYING SNOOPERS

PREDICTION 1940 **The huge mechanical ears that the army uses to detect distant airplanes** require from eight to ten men to operate. In recent California tests, an untended robot ear was tried out for the first time. Guarding a lonely mountain pass more than 100 miles away, the ear picked up the sound of the invading planes as they passed overhead and transmitted it along a power line as carrier current to the message center. The cathode tube gave a visual sound track of the flying planes, permitting detection and identification of the type at long distance. Ultimately, the robot listening post may be improved to report the altitude, direction of flight, and even the number of planes that it "hears."

PREDICTION 1943 **Clipping the treetops at 5 miles a minute, the pilot of a Yankee pursuit plane pulls the trigger.** But no rattle of machine guns follows, no bullets rip the hangars flanking the enemy airfield over which he skims. This is a photographic strafer. The trigger starts a roll of film unwinding, and the plane brings home a continuous-strip picture of everything within range. There has been no warning of the approach of the low-flying plane, and anti-aircraft weapons are virtually useless against it in the seconds that it is overhead. (*Continued on page 67.*)

During the first few months of the war Paris was repeatedly besieged by German airplanes. A former head of the aeronautical department was recalled to the capital to devise a system of protection, and the present scheme is the result. Essentially this little detector consists of four large megaphones, all of which point in the same direction. These devices are connected to a microphone which amplifies the faintest of sounds gathered by the wide-mouthed horns.

Back at his base, the flying snooper's film is processed into a continuous photograph; no overlapping of separate views, no tedious study of faint outlines magnified from a high-altitude shot. The low-level picture is sharp in every detail despite the terrific speed at which it was filmed.

A second innovation is a continuous-strip printer that can produce 1,000 9-by-9 inch prints per hour, a rate many times faster than standard photo-printing machines. Two men can do the job, and they need no air-conditioned laboratory: the portable machine can be operated in an army tent.

 PREDICTION 1928 These super-sensitive sound collectors are the "ears" of self-aiming anti-aircraft guns that track airplanes by sound.

PREDICTION 1956 Army combat commanders can peer over enemy lines with a TV camera mounted in a remotely controlled plane. An L-17 is fitted with a 42-pound autopilot that enables a ground operator to regulate its flight, landings, and takeoffs within a 25-mile range. TV pictures of strategic territory beneath the plane are relayed to a monitor set at the 250-pound ground station, which can be carried in a jeep. It includes radio links for commanding the drone. Still photos can also be made.

Combat aerial photos in future wars will be taken without risking the lives of pilots or aerial photographers. A small radio-controlled, camera-carrying drone developed by the U.S. Army Signal Corps will make this possible. The drone, officially designated as the RP-71, can operate in all kinds of weather, and take still or motion pictures anywhere from several hundred feet to more than four miles above the earth. One big advantage of the drone is that it requires no airfields from which to operate, since it is jetted from a portable launching catapult. Once in the air, however, it is propeller-driven by a gasoline motor. A control operator on the ground guides the craft to its destination and back. Then the engine is stopped and the drone comes down by parachute. With it, tactical commanders can have aerial photos in less than an hour.

PREDICTION 1957 "Red leader—vector one-nine-zero—angels two-zero, over." The crisp order containing flight instructions for a formation of interceptor planes came loud and clear from a black box in a

Long Island laboratory. There was an eerie quality to the voice. Each word sounded as though a different person said it. Eeriest of all, though, was that no human being had put that message together or spoken it: the words had been plucked electronically from a canned vocabulary, pieced together, and broadcast in proper sequence.

The weird "voice" is, in effect, a set of "vocal cords" that allows an electronic brain to say what it is "thinking" in any language! Known as Automatic Voice Data Link, the compact unit can take output signals from an electronic computer and translate them instantly into a series of verbal messages that can be broadcast to flying aircraft or put out over a public-address system.

The inventor, Charles Poppe, envisions dozens of other uses for the unique voice. It could become a link between a computer and the radar operator, spitting out data while he watches the scope. It may some day enable automatic weather stations to shout their reports via radio to all points of the globe in a dozen different languages. Inventory memory computers may talk to accountants in vast industrial organizations, giving accounts of stock on hand. Oil company engineers, to find the level of any tank in farms spread across the country, will only need to dial a phone number. Huge electronic brains, collecting tank-level data from the entire system continually, will feed the necessary impulses to

a Voice Data Link, which will, in plain English, tell the engineer the level of any tank in the entire system at any time.

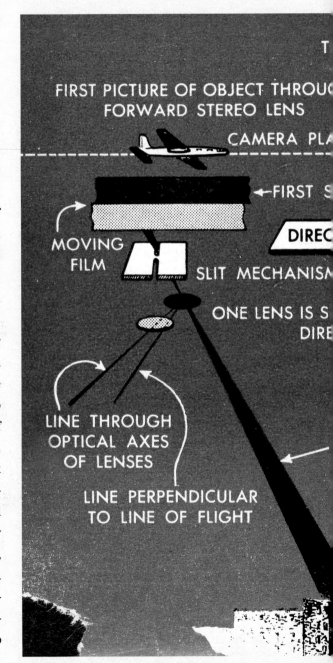

FIRST PICTURE OF OBJECT THROUG
FORWARD STEREO LENS

CAMERA PL

←FIRST S

DIREC

SLIT MECHANISM

ONE LENS IS S
DIRE

MOVING
FILM

LINE THROUGH
OPTICAL AXES
OF LENSES

LINE PERPENDICULAR
TO LINE OF FLIGHT

So far, neither Poppe, nor any of his cohorts has figured what will happen if somebody asks an electronic brain a silly question. Possibly a sarcastic word or two will be programmed into the revolving vocabulary to respond to clowns.

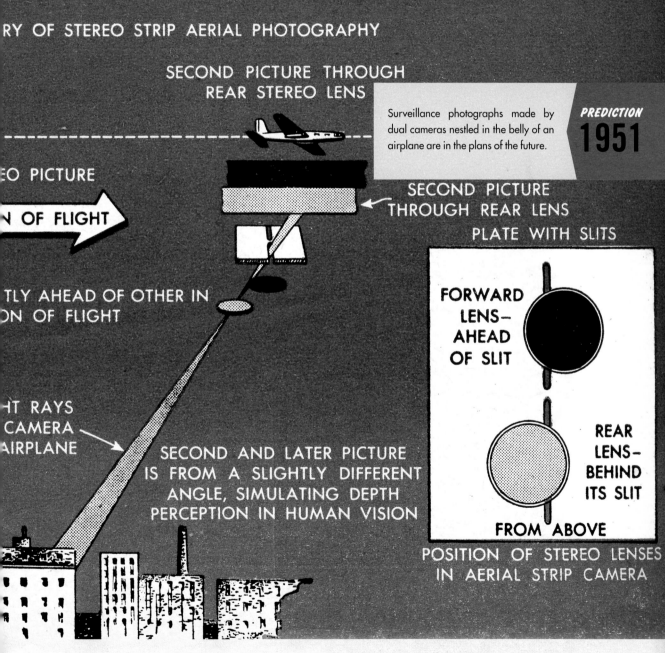

...RY OF STEREO STRIP AERIAL PHOTOGRAPHY

SECOND PICTURE THROUGH
REAR STEREO LENS

...EO PICTURE

...N OF FLIGHT

...TLY AHEAD OF OTHER IN
...ON OF FLIGHT

...HT RAYS
...CAMERA
...AIRPLANE

Surveillance photographs made by dual cameras nestled in the belly of an airplane are in the plans of the future.

PREDICTION
1951

SECOND PICTURE
THROUGH REAR LENS
PLATE WITH SLITS

FORWARD LENS— AHEAD OF SLIT

REAR LENS— BEHIND ITS SLIT

FROM ABOVE

POSITION OF STEREO LENSES IN AERIAL STRIP CAMERA

SECOND AND LATER PICTURE IS FROM A SLIGHTLY DIFFERENT ANGLE, SIMULATING DEPTH PERCEPTION IN HUMAN VISION

PREDICTION 1960 Lloyd E. Snapp of Combat Surveillance and Avionics says the company is developing drones that can fly long-range missions. After they leave local radio control they fly a preprogrammed flight, changing altitude and direction according to preset instructions, eventually returning to local control.

Meanwhile, they take pictures. The camera on the drone adjusts its diaphragm according to the amount of light, changes focus automatically depending on the distance to the ground, uses image motion compensation to offset the drone's speed, and employs powerful flash cartridges for after-dark work—all automatically.

The drone develops its own pictures in the air and uses an optical transducer to convert the images into electrical impulses that are radioed back to base. There a receiving camera converts the impulses into finished prints and at the same time produces a transparency that can be looked at in a viewer. This all happens in the space of three minutes while the drone may be several hundred miles away and traveling at twice the speed of sound at extremely high altitude!

Another new development is a TV system that doesn't blur at high speed and can therefore be mounted in a drone, radioing its pictures back to a viewing tube on the ground. The "side-looking" radar also can be mounted on a drone, as can infrared surveillance devices.

PREDICTION 1963 Even experts are awed by the precision of the remarkable cameras that exposed Khruschev's dirty work in Cuba. Automatic machines that measure the length of a photographed runway or the height of a missile on its launching pad reduce hours of calculations to seconds for photo-interpreters who know how high the recon plane was flying and the focal length of the camera that took the picture.

Even more fantastic equipment is under development and will presently join the surveillance designed to prevent future Cubas or Pearl Harbors. Soon, completely electronic photo-reading machines will scan hundreds of photographs per minute and ring bells whenever a new photo shows something that was not in an older shot of the same scene. Photo-sensors that are partly television sets and partly infrared cameras will make night seem like day for aerial photographers.

ROBOT CREWS FLY THE AIRLINERS

PREDICTION 1945 Robot flight crews will do most of the work of flying the post-war airliners. The human pilots and co-pilots are simply commanders-in-chief who direct the labors of their mechanical employees.

Such a flight crew consists of 100 or more different mechanisms, electric or hydraulic, each of which is built to do one

"FLYING JEEPS" SKIM OBSTACLES IN LAYING WIRE

Light "grasshopper" planes lay wires across any type of terrain. In the near future, the lives of our men in uniform won't be at risk as these planes may be replaced by radio-controlled drone aircraft.

job correctly and rapidly. The robot crew of the B-29, forerunner of the 100-passenger Boeing Stratocruiser that has crossed the continent in six hours and three minutes, consists almost entirely of electric motors. Even the 7,000-pound landing gear of the B-29 is retracted by electric motors. Its electronic automatic pilot can make as many as 300 flight corrections per minute. The only hydraulic device on the plane is a booster for applying the brakes. The robots that do the work on the Douglas C-54 Skymaster, on the other hand, are nearly all actuated by hydraulic force.

A few of the 152 electric motors that power the B-29 are shown. This plane is the first of its kind, and in the post-war air, human pilots and co-pilots will direct their mechanical employees, like the ¼ horsepower motor held by the young lady.

FUTURE TEACHING MACHINES
WILL INSTRUCT THE ARMED FORCES IN TACTICS

Education in America today is timorously facing a mechanical revolution. The catalyst is a device unfortunately labeled the "teaching machine." At the moment, it comes in widely variegated sizes and shapes. It is not new, but educators and textbook manufacturers who have long regarded the teaching machine as a gadget are taking a second, serious look at it. A rash of experimental machine teaching is appearing in schools all over the nation. Early results indicate an exciting educational potential.

Few will dispute the value of machine- teaching in the armed forces and industry. The air force is making increasing use of them to instruct technicians in subjects ranging from aircraft mechanics to guided missiles. Machines (psychomotor self-instructional devices) are proving remarkably effective teachers of such motor skills as typing and punch-press operation.

3

AIRPLANES WILL REPLACE CAVALRY

Despite optimistic stories like 1910's "Battleships Face Down Air Fleets," air power was the sizzle that sold the steak of all tech warfare throughout the 20th century. While aircraft alone seldom decided wars, they changed the terms of debate and captured the imagination of generals and the public alike. The age-old desire of humans for flight swiftly migrated to their innate propensity to fight.

In 1907, a rear admiral still waxed enthusiastically about the airship's possibilities as a weapon of war against cities, but doubted that a flying machine would ever rival naval fighters. Up until the 1930s, he was right—but thereafter aircraft carriers dominated naval war, the central queen bees to swarms of support ships. The vastly greater speeds of airplanes decided the issue, as they could strike at greater distances and command the skies.

In 1912's article "Wood Takes to the Air," we see the beginnings of an idea that would finally die with the famous Spruce Goose (actually constructed of birch), which had exactly one flight in 1947 before becoming a museum exhibit. In 1942 would-be aviators tried plastic, and the United States used wooden gliders in the Normandy landings.

This use of light but weak materials held true until metal planes with larger engines capable of larger engines and far high speeds came along. By that time it became clear "the cities themselves are attacked directly by high explosive bombs and gas." Even though the 1929 Geneva Convention ruled out the use of gas, savvy types thought it would be used anyway—and most nations armed themselves under that assumption. That gas warfare did not occur during World War II is one of the few examples of mutual fear driving humanitarian concerns—that is, until the nuclear standoff of the 1950s to the present.

Airplanes captured the zip and joy of flight much better than balloons. *Popular Mechanics* wondered "Who Said the Blimp is All Through?" in 1929, just eight years before the footage and passionate recording of the Hindenburg explosion shattered the public's and industry's faith in airships. The media made such disasters matter, although there were more than twice the fatalities when a helium-filled United States Navy scout airship crashed at sea off the New Jersey coast merely four years earlier. Perception is everything.

Envisioned by da Vinci centuries before, the wingless aircraft of 1914 (also called "autogyros") became the workhorse helicopters of the battlefield. The English called a similar craft the Flying Tea-tray.

The gigantic zeppelin airships planned in the future will cost not less than one-third of a million dollars each, and over $1,000 for a single filling of hydrogen gas.

An exceptionally large wing area enables the U.S. Army Air Force's first all-metal liaison plane to take off or land within 230 feet and be towed in the air like a glider—without removing the propeller. The right-hand controls are removable to convert the plane into an ambulance for two patients besides the pilot as well as an attendant.

While helicopters didn't have practical use as a bomber, they delivered troops and supplies, and offered rocket and machine gun support. Perhaps the most amusing detail buried in these *Popular Mechanics* articles is a quote from inventor Igor Sikorsky, the most important figure in helicopter development, who said in 1959: "One day you will see helicopters, with automatic detachable hooks dangling under them. They will be 'elevators' for small airplanes—hoisting them from small parking places in forests or Jungles and releasing them at high altitudes." This proposal ran into so many problems it was never attempted.

Other ideas, such as the small and compact Christie flying tank (weighing a mere 11,000 pounds), failed as well. It's easy to guess now that a 1930 machine with the "features of an amphibian, a dirigible, a gyropter and an ordinary airplane" might not work out. Such predictions fail to account for the lapses of blueprint prophecy—leaping forward from a basic design, while failing to see how machines that seem to do everything, do nothing well.

Interestingly, both the United States and the Soviet Union developed atomic rockets. The United States tested for 100 hours their NERVA (Nuclear Engine for Rocket Vehicle Application) and the Soviets ran theirs 1000 hours in a cavern, finding very little radioactivity in the plume. These had so much thrust they could haul enough shielding mass (or just place the propulsion far from the people).

Politics killed both those innovations, but they remain readily available for the exploration and development of our solar system, where chemical rockets have largely reached their limits. Nuclear rockets are at least twice as effective in lifting mass as the best chemical (oxygen plus hydrogen) rockets in use, such as the Apollo and Space Shuttle systems. The NERVA system sits in a Nevada warehouse, waiting for its future to arrive.

Popular Mechanics explored all these possibilities, thinking forward to the seemingly inevitable wars to come. ◎

THE NEXT WAR IN THE AIR

PREDICTION 1907 **Do balloons and airships have practical value in war?** Rear Admiral Sigsbee says: "The airship may in time prove a dangerous enemy by dropping explosives into a city, but as a force against naval fighters it will never do."

But Rear Admiral Chester disagrees: "We old fellows have seen the sailing vessel give way to the armor-clad steam warships, and I predict that the future will see the airplane fighting machine. The airplane is the fighting machine of the future."

PREDICTION 1909 **Roy Knabenshue sailed over Los Angeles** on the night of December 18, 1908, and dropped confetti bombs onto the heads of the thousands of people who thronged the business district to try to see him. After "blowing up" the city hall and the greater part of the business district, Knabenshue made a trip around the residential portions of the city, traveling in all about 18 miles in one and a half hours.

The test was considered conclusive: a fleet of airships could easily destroy a city without danger to the aerial fighters themselves. Airships can, and will, in the next great war, play a great part in engagements on the battlefield and in bombarding fortifications, but whether they can be used without serious danger of being destroyed by the enemy they are attacking has yet to be proved.

PREDICTION 1915 **After eight months of war it is now possible to form an estimate of the true value of airplanes in naval and military operations.**

Most people thought that bombs would only be dropped as a means of annoying the enemy and not as a serious attempt to do material damage. However, aerial bombings have proven quite effective. It is evident that a machine gun mounted on an airplane can be an efficient weapon, though there is the obvious difficulty of siting a machine gun so that the stream of bullets does not hit the propeller. The French tried fixing the gun so high up on a monoplane that it cleared the propeller tip, but the passenger had to stand up to fire, which was exceedingly uncomfortable for him, considering that he was plowing through the air at over 60 miles per hour, and consequently his shooting was apt to be more erratic than effective.

The opinion of those military people who believed that aircraft would hasten the end of the first war in which they were employed has been entirely disproved. Aircraft can spot everybody's maneuvers, making it impossible to mass troops at any one point without the opposing commander being able to mass sufficient troops to respond. So after all, our latest invention as a weapon of war brings us back to the most primitive fighting of all: man-to-man frontal attack.

In the dogfights of the future, the pilot and the gunner will work together to function in midair.

PREDICTION 1930

PREDICTION 1931 **Balloon aces were very scarce during the war,** for those intrepid flyers who went in for "busting" captive balloons lived short and exciting lives. Even on peacetime balloon-bursting maneuvers, death hovers in the vicinity of the big gas bags. By holding a dive too long, a pilot may fly into the bag, or he may scrape it and tangle a wing, or it may explode in his face and surround him with flaming hydrogen gas.

The fast pursuit planes gain a great altitude above the balloon. Then the pilot sticks the nose straight down and lets the slim white marker on the airspeed indicator climb against the peg. When close to the balloon, small bombs are released or machine-gun fire is opened up, and the pilot pulls carefully out of the dive just at the right time and place. The trick is not easy to do.

Most pilots find themselves pulling out of the dive too early. It takes the most practiced judgment to determine the right moment to pull out. No censure is attached to a pilot's pulling off too quickly, but if he holds his dive too long and fouls the bag, he is usually soon beyond any worldly censure.

In the next war these balloons will be protected by far more efficient anti-aircraft guns. The man who gets balloons in future wars must travel so fast that he can scarcely be seen.

PREDICTION 1931 Observers from balloons directed artillery fire with great effect during World War I, and we can expect these balloons to be present in the next war.

WHO SAID THE BLIMP IS ALL THROUGH?

PREDICTION 1929 **The navy has ordered two giant dirigibles,** larger than any yet built, and this sketch shows how they will compare to a battleship. Note the gun turret on the side and others on top near the bow and stern; the guns will be used to repel airplane attacks.

PREDICTION 1942 **Rigid airships, each carrying ten attack bombing planes and capable of ranging thousands of miles from their bases,** might be employed effectively by the United States Navy, according to lighter-than-aircraft experts. These flying carriers would operate in conjunction with other units of the navy, including aircraft carriers. Immune, of course, to submarine attack, the airship would be expected to operate beyond the range of land-based enemy planes and at altitudes above the effective gun range of surface vessels. In case of attack, it would be able to take refuge in the clouds while its own planes streamed out to meet the enemy. (see page 85 for visual.)

PREDICTION 1958 **The new airships will have to be large,** for they will carry the heaviest array of radar equipment ever sent into the skies to watch for possible invaders. Each ship will hold 1.5 million cubic feet of helium, 50 percent more than the capacity of the biggest blimp that had previously been in service, and will be close to two city blocks long. In such military work as anti-submarine patrolling and early-warning watching, airships are said to be less expensive than comparable heavier-than-air units.

VERTICAL HOVERING FLIGHT NOW AN ACCOMPLISHED FACT

PREDICTION 1909 **An English aerial critic,** looking at the great surface of the airplane exposed to the elements, noted that it is a fair-weather machine only, and as such has little, if any, commercial value. He stated that a combination helicopter and airplane will be the future flying-machine, on account of its being able to take off and land vertically, thus requiring no special starting or alighting place.

Another English critic, in an article in the *London Motor*, differs with his compatriot, insisting that the airplane is only in its infancy and subject to many changes that will overcome the obstacles mentioned. The future airplane, he believes, will carry a device for launching itself off the ground like a rocket, without any special preparations.

DIRIGIBLE "MOTHER SHIPS" *HOLD DOZENS OF PLANES*

Soon planes will be launched and retrieved by airships. Launching is accomplished by lowering the plane, attached to a sort of trapeze bar by means of a hook, through a trapdoor. Then, with the plane's motor or motors roaring, the pilot releases the hook and the plane drops away.

Independent of vast airfields and incorporating many other desirable characteristics, the wingless aircraft seems on the verge of development into an important weapon of defensive—perhaps even offensive—warfare.

With sufficient funds made available, it should be possible to produce an autogyro with much greater payloads than are available today. Protected by armor from enemy gunfire, able to give a good account of itself by means of cannons mounted in the ship, and powered by engines able to give it the necessary load-carrying capacity, such an autogyro would be of practical use as a bomber because it could operate in cases of low ceiling, when planes would be helpless.

To interpose an effective defense against bombers or dive bombers, the helicopter is ideal. It can remain still in the air, thus affording a stable gun emplacement from which the gunner can await the moment—which must come either in bombing from altitude or while dive bombing—when the bomber ceases all zigzag maneuvering and flies a perfectly straight line for its quarry. Then the bomber is comparatively easy to hit. The helicopter, of course, can easily achieve an altitude of up to 15,000 feet or more and can carry large-caliber machine guns or even cannons.

PREDICTION 1921

CAPTIVE HELICOPTERS
TO REPLACE BALLOONS

Designed as a substitute for the captive observation balloon, this three-engine helicopter is not intended for horizontal flight. A monster parachute having a surface of 2,690 feet is permanently attached to the machine's center shaft. Should two engines fail, which is most unlikely, the remaining one, aided by the huge parachute, will, it is thought, permit the heavy apparatus to drop gently to earth.

A West Coast designer foresees rotary-wing "tugs" lowering and lifting tomorrow's fighters into and out of small landing sites such as the cramped decks of ships.

PREDICTION
1953

PREDICTION 1944 **A speed of 300 miles per hour and comparatively unlimited ceiling are predicted** for the helicopters of the future. They would be made of synthetic bonded plywood, plastics, and steel tubing. The single-rotor models would have the advantage of more economical construction and lighter weight than the two-rotor craft, but the latter would have much greater lift. Although most of the models are built to accommodate four persons, one military version provides for two pilots and four 200-pound depth bombs. Jet propulsion is believed to be the ultimate in helicopter development, but it will probably be several years before this principle is successfully adapted.

PREDICTION 1959 **"One day,"** predicts inventor Igor Sikorsky, **"you will see helicopters with automatic detachable hooks** dangling under them. They will be 'elevators' for small airplanes—hoisting them from small parking places in forests or jungles and releasing them at high altitudes. They could also hook such planes in midair and lower them into areas where they could otherwise never land.

"Jets may be applied to rotor tips for better performance," he adds. "And you will see great advancement made in flying cranes—for hoisting movable-pod buildings to battlefields and construction sites as well as lifting great steel assemblies to places no crane can reach."

England's huge new experimental heli-copters can hold about 100 troops and lift jeeps and tanks.

PREDICTION
1952

What about those ducted fans and flying platforms? "If the fan stops," Sikorsky points out with a humorous twinkle in his eye, "you then have a choice. I call it the 'two Ps'—for 'parachute or pray.' And you pray not for your safety but for your ultimate destination."

WINGLESS PLANES PREDICTED AS RESULT OF ARMY TESTS

PREDICTION 1914 **A curious-looking monoplane, popularly known in Great Britain as the Flying Teatray,** is built ring-shaped, the idea being that it would right itself automatically if it capsized. Correctly speaking, the wings are curved backward to join with the tail, which is enlarged, thus completing a circle. Extending through the center of the ring and joining its two rims is the body, which differs little from that of an ordinary monoplane. Odd-looking plane surfaces and fins at the rear of the machine provide elevators and a rudder. The craft is still in the experimental stage, but has made several interesting flights and attracted considerable comment on account of its peculiar appearance.

PREDICTION 1926 **Motors that can propel airplanes** without the lifting power of the wing surfaces have been developed, army tests disclose. Pursuit airplanes of the future will literally be winged projectiles—mostly engine and propeller, and with wings of the minimum length and surface required for taking off, steering, and banking.

PREDICTION 1932 **Small, compact, grim, and ugly, the Christie flying tank** weighs 11,000 pounds. It may be the fuselage of a plane whose wings are released when the tank touches the ground and goes into action, or carried by large planes and released instead of bombs. A 750-horse-power engine may either be used to drive the tank forward or turn the propeller for flying. When a flying tank takes off, its driving wheels gather so much momentum within the first 80 to 90 yards that when the power is transferred to the propeller, the tank will go into the air within 100. And the pilot of a flying tank, like that of a helicopter, does not need the level ground required by a bombing plane to take off.

WOOD TAKES TO THE AIR

PREDICTION 1912 **The materials used for future airplanes are likely to remain much the same as at present.** Fabric would seem superior—in strength, durability, and ease of application—to wood and sheet metal, sometimes proposed as substitutes for it for wing surfacing. The use of fabric for the sails of boats, which involves analogous requirements, is rather suggestive on this score.

Wood also possesses superlative merits, and although steel may supplant it for wing bars and some elements of the framing, wood is likely to persist for a long time in rib construction, and bodywork.

PREDICTION 1941 **A corrosion-proof metal like stainless steel could not be confined to cutlery.** The aviation industry has found it useful in dozens of applications, such as fire walls between engine and pilot's compartment, elevator frames, ailerons, fuel tanks, tail booms, rudder frames, and even entire wings. Fighting and bombing planes include much stainless steel; not far in the future may be all-stainless-steel aircraft. (*Continued on page 95.*)

PREDICTION 1932 Flying tanks can take off through mud or bumpy ground that would prevent the average plane from rising.

Flying Tank — Newest Air Menace

This proposed "convertiplane" will take off like a helicopter and drive forward like an airplane.

From electric furnaces, like this one at the Carnegie-Illinois Steel Corporation, come the tough materials necessary in modern war machines.

ROTATING WING *CAN ACT AS PARACHUTE*

Features of an amphibian, a dirigible, a gyropter, and an ordinary airplane are incorporated in this flying machine. The craft has a pair of single-bladed wings, a rotating disk-shaped affair filled with gas or hot air. Quarters for crew and passengers are arranged on either side of the central machinery. The body has retractable wheels so that the ship can be landed on the ground or on water. In descents, the rotating wing is intended to act as a parachute.

PREDICTION 1943 Workers join the halves of the fuselage shell for a plastic-plywood aircraft.

One plant is building a glider with a fuselage of tubular steel covered by long-fiber cotton fabric and with wings of aircraft spruce and mahogany plywood. Others of the new air types now in production contain virtually nothing but wood.

Riveted metal surfaces become wrinkled and rough, with consequent loss of performance. Aircraft manufacturer Sherman M. Fairchild declares, "All our investigations led to the use of fibers—preferably wood fibers—in the form of veneers bound together and protected by plastics. This is a new material with great structural and aerodynamic advantages."

Otto W. Timm, president of the Timm Aircraft Corporation, believes plastic-plywood craft may be easily built and repaired using existing woodworking plants and their craftsmen, and the unlimited sources of supply. Plywood is more fire-resistant than magnesium or aluminum, and also corrosion-resistant—of particular value in naval aircraft and in aircraft for tropical assignments.

PREDICTION 1945 **Look back a quarter of a century, when it was considered impossible to build an airplane of metal.** Now our engineers have even advanced the idea of a glass airplane, which may never be needed, but the plastic plane is a practical prospect soon after the war. Already there is an experimental, and flyable, model with plastic fuselage and wings. Plastics may be the answer to the "air flivver" problem, providing cheap, strong materials for Mr. Average Man's airplane.

AN INDISPENSIBLE AERONAUTIC APPARATUS

PREDICTION 1914 **A gyroscopic apparatus recently invented and patented** apparently places at the disposal of the airman a complete and reliable means for controlling all the operations of balancing, banking, and steering an airplane. The apparatus consists of two gyroscopes mounted on the same vertical axis and revolving in opposite directions. By means of control wheels, the airman can bring about either motion quickly and to any degree required, and since the gyroscopes retain their original plane of rotation, either action results simply in tilting the airplane in the direction desired.

PREDICTION 1915 **It has been recommended by the chief signal officer that parachutes be purchased** for members of the army aviation service. This step was taken following tests at the San Diego aeronautic station, where a young woman made a successful drop of 1,800 feet from an airplane. The parachute is light, compact, and so made that it may be folded and

PREDICTION 1928 So that the jumper may more easily guide himself while falling through the air, this fin arrangement has been designed for the parachute man.

strapped to a machine's occupant in such a way that it does not interfere with his normal movements.

BOMBARDIER WATCHES INDISTINCT IMAGE OF TARGET ON SCREEN

ELECTRONIC BEAM TRAVELS THROUGH CLOUD AND IS ECHOED FROM TARGET TO CATHODE RAY TUBE IN PLANE

PREDICTION 1942 Flight recorders such as those being used in England to locate and track invading planes promise to become a useful safety measure in the future. The principles of the flight recorder may also be applied to determining the positions of fog-bound ships, for locating submarines underwater, and even for learning the exact locations of all the police radio cars in a large city.

PREDICTION 1945 One of the cherished secrets of the American and Royal Air Forces is the method by which bombardiers find invisible targets through heavy overcast. Enough has been told now to indicate that this electronic eye developed from a marriage of radar and television: the bomb aimer, watching the face of a cathode ray tube, sees the general outlines of the hidden target sketched by the radio signals beamed downward from the transmitter and echoed back to the tube in the little black box. The bombardier can recognize a particular objective by its shadowy shape on the fluorescent screen. Meanwhile, the attacking bombers are hidden from defending fighter planes and antiaircraft batteries.

PREDICTION 1945 A bombardier uses a combination of radar and television to "see" through clouds to the targets below.

Huge gliders carry tanks and troops behind enemy lines.

PREDICTION 1956 Some research experts of the Civil Aeronautics Administration predict that every air transport will be equipped with two periscopes in the years immediately ahead. One periscope will have an "eye" in the bottom of the plane's fuselage, while the other would searches sky above. A single observer would operate both, one at a time, inspecting the areas below and above the plane, and at the sides and the rear. A dial on the pilot's instrument panel would show him just where the periscope "eye" was looking. When the periscope observer sighted an approaching plane, he would press a button to signal the pilot who, by looking at the dial, could tell where the neighboring plane was flying.

DESIGNING TOMORROW'S AIRPLANES

PREDICTION 1912 Just as surely as there has been an almost biological evolution of the steamship and the railway must there ultimately disappear the freak forms of (and the more freakish substitutes for) the one soundly conceived, really progressing vehicle of the skies. We may dismiss from present consideration such follies as the gasbag and the thin-surfaced, wire-encumbered, bodyless types of airplanes as of no continuing interest—except as bottomless sinks into which to plunge labor and capital, and murderous devices with which to slaughter the foolish and reckless.

The airplane of the future, to be designed soundly and built well, must be substantially a gigantic bird. The controls of the future machine are likely to become purely directional rather than stabilizing, making them measurably surer in operation and somewhat simpler to manipulate. The motors of the future machines will almost certainly be placed in front. Structural integrity must be secured in the future airplane as positively as it is in high-grade automobiles. The airplane of the future may be reasonably expected to present only a few heavy and streamlined cables, in place of the multitude of line wires so generally employed nowadays.

Instead of the reckless flying that has become so common with half-developed machines—flying from the roofs of buildings, under the bridge at Niagara Falls, and so on—there may be expected a safe and sane flying from large, prepared land or smooth water areas from selected start to specified destination.

The high efficiency of the machines of the future will make high reliability more important in motors than light weight and extreme power, so the airplane motor will probably always remain substantially a close counterpart of the internal combustion motors in motorboats and automobiles.

The question of speed can be very well left to rest on present accomplishments.

The Russians are experimenting with tow trains of gliders that could silently carry troops more than 100 miles after being cut loose from a powered airplane.

Already one French monoplane has repeatedly proved capable of a speed of 105 miles per hour. The airplane of the future will doubtlessly be faster, but if it even remains only as fast—probably with less power than is now required—its utility, insofar as this relates to speed, will be superior to that of all other vehicles.

PREDICTION 1942 **One development that promises to influence future aeronautical design is the Davis wing.** Developed by D. R. Davis, this new long-range wing shape reduces drag, to some extent taking the brakes off airfoil sections. Its use makes aircraft as much as 15 percent more efficient.

PREDICTION 1954 **Looking into the future, aircraft engineers agree** that it is going to take much more than an advanced wing and a big power plant to achieve supersonic speeds. The big problem is preventing the aircraft from literally burning up while flying fast. Aerodynamic heating from friction with the air is already a problem at today's fast cruising speeds. Complex and relatively heavy refrigeration equipment must be installed in fighter aircraft to keep the electronic systems and the human pilot at safe operating temperatures.

THE GREAT FUTURE OF WORLD AIR TRANSPORT

PREDICTION 1927 **Colonel John A. Paegelow believes there is a good future** in lighter-than-air ships for a young enlistee of good physique and a good education, particularly in mathematics. The future lies not only in the service, but in the commercial airship lines, which he believes are sure to come within a few years, particularly for long routes across the ocean.

Already, enlisted men who qualify as mechanics are proving so popular with commercial flying companies that many are being bought out of the service to earn good salaries with private concerns.

PREDICTION 1935 **Pan-American Airways plans to span the Pacific with a $2 million fleet of six mammoth clippers,** the first of which has already gone into experimental service. With the use of the clippers, the post office is contemplating a six-day mail service between Shanghai and New York.

The London-Shanghai route can be completed within three days, making possible a ten-day tour of the globe, if connections can be made without delays. This is less than one-fifth the time required at present and one-eighth the time that Jules Verne predicted.

PREDICTION
1941 **The wings of the big planes of the future will be so thick** that we will be able to place many engines on each propeller shaft, using 10,000 horsepower or several times that amount to turn each propeller.

The 500-passenger airplane, or a plane of two or three times that capacity will be built as soon as there is a need for it. Such planes will have room enough inside for passengers to dance their way across country to the music of the plane's own orchestra.

PREDICTION
1932 When the transport airplane of the future meets with disaster in flight, a giant parachute will lift the detachable cabin from the disabled plane and lower the passengers to earth.

PREDICTION 1942 **The very instruments by which we locate hostile aircraft** and assail them will ensure both air and surface craft safe passage in any weather. We all read of the soldier, on watch at Pearl Harbor the morning of December 7, who clamored into deaf ears that there were airplanes 150 miles from his post. Imagine such a power devoted, by airplanes and ships, to detecting navigational hazards many miles away without depending on visual or audible warning signals.

Or consider another device by which we see through fog. Grim enough when we know it is used by fighting pilots fingering triggers in wait for the enemy planes thus spotted. But it would be a blessing for the commercial pilot coming in for a landing with his precious freight of human lives.

PREDICTION 1943 **The glider pickup and discharge system offers great promise** in serving small communities without airports. This development, already well established for air mail, should become of tremendous value when all first-class mail goes by air. From there it should go into air express and, provided pickup accelerations can be kept at reasonable "g's," into passenger travel. The glider train definitely appears to offer economies in cost per ton mile of goods carried, compared with concentrated loading in the powered plane.

Progress has created another problem that engineering must consider. It involves assisted takeoff acceleration and perhaps landing acceleration. We are constantly running wing loadings higher, but airports can't grow much more: so either wing loadings will have to stop, or assisted takeoff by gravity, catapult, rocket, or other device will have to be developed.

PREDICTION 1956

ATOMIC-POWERED
JET TRANSPORT OF THE FUTURE

Commercial airliners using atomic power are only 10 years away. We can expect an atomic airliner to be some 200 feet long, with a delta wing and a long fuselage. It will weigh 150 to 250 tons and will cruise at 60,000 feet, at a speed of 1,500 miles per hour or more; 35 to 50 tons of shielding would protect the crew and passengers. Atomic airliners will be able to cruise around and around the earth, staying aloft for weeks or months at a time.

We shall also have in the peace many, many airfields built for war and then made available to commerce. Aviation should then take its proper place in the transportation and private travel picture. It is unlikely to ever touch $9/10$ths of the transportation now carried by rail, road, and water. However, it will create new opportunities for trade and stimulate new desires to travel.

Each prominent airport should become a beehive of industry in itself. All modern air terminals already have many auxiliary businesses—newsstands, barber shops, lunchrooms—and in some cases branch banks, haberdashery stores, and other shops. And certainly every airport in the future must have a large garage and drive-yourself system. A car rental bureau at every airport would mean that a businessman could walk directly from his airliner to the car station, make his business calls by automobile, and return to the airport ready to fly the next portion of his trip. Fanciful, yes—but altogether possible!

PREDICTION 1952 Atomic energy may fly airplanes in the next generation. Somebody alive today may take a voyage in a spaceship. Experiments with guided missiles may result in drastic changes in our aircraft. An airframe not even on the drawing boards today may be the conventional design at the close of this century. Tomorrow's multijet airliner at 150,000-foot altitude could travel from New York to Miami in 15 minutes. If you're talking about airplanes, it's wise not to scoff at anything.

PREDICTION 1934 This artist's conception of how rockets will be guided in their flights in space depicts pilots strapped in a sealed compartment.

PREDICTION 1963
Setting our sights on Mach-3 will be tremendously expensive. Development of the triple-sonic airliner may run to $1 billion for the first one and perhaps $20 million per copy after the billion is spent in research. To operate economically, an airline might have to charge $1,000 or even $2,500 for a round-trip across-the-country flight. The planes would fly empty.

But national prestige demands that we build Mach-3 airliners even though their cost can't be justified on economic grounds. Uncle Sam will just have to pick up most of the check.

Once upon a time, piston-engine aircraft used to cart us across the country in 8 hours—plus. Five years ago, the jets chopped this time to eight hours, or less. That was really traveling, it seemed at first, but now experienced air travelers are becoming bored. They can hardly wait to go supersonic!

PREDICTION 1947
Highly streamlined new rocket planes will be the first to break the sound barrier.

4

AT HOME ON
LAND OR
WATER

U nlike submarines, tanks are dramatic; it's part of their appeal. They roll forward with implacable potency, engines roaring, machine guns hammering, treads clanking. They are moving symbols of the frightening impersonal inhumanity of modern warfare: *machines hunting men*. To strategists, they eliminate from view the soft humans tucked inside, who are still vulnerable to armor-piercing munitions.

On the other hand, submarines strike without being seen. There's little foreboding threat until a torpedo is suddenly arrowing in at a ship. They too shelter men, cowering beneath the depths and protected inside steel-supported, bottled-air compartments.

Both these modern modes of warfare emerged from the imaginations of science fiction writers. Jules Verne penned *20,000 Leagues Beneath the Sea* (not a depth, but the distance the sub covered) soon after hearing of the first small subs built by both sides in the Civil War. Verne's *Nautilus* sinks warships and is a champion of the world's underdogs and downtrodden, a revolutionary idea in 1869. Submarines attacking warships seemed their obvious use, although in the largest ocean conflict to date, World War II, they mostly sank poorly defended merchant ships.

Few works are as uncannily accurate in foretelling the future as "The Land Ironclads," a short story published in 1903

Some of the 70,000 workers at the New York Navy Yard in Brooklyn are women, and in the future, more women will be support staff for our boys overseas. Here those welders are hard at work on the flight deck.

PREDICTION
1945

by H.G. Wells. (While Leonardo da Vinci had also designed a proto-tank, Wells' chief inspiration seems to have been ironclad ships, which also feature significantly in one scene from *The War of the Worlds*.) Winston Churchill recalled this tale during World War I and jumpstarted the research leading to its use on the battlefield. He even named the project the Landships Committee.

Well's short story portrays conflicts remarkably similar to the trench warfare

PREDICTION 1931 One of the chief obstacles to long-distance flights has been in getting into the air at the start. The plane is loaded with its necessary pay burden, that is, the mail, express, or passengers it must carry; then, in addition to this, it carries gasoline and oil. The take-off is often a hazardous and trying affair.

stalemate of World War I, in which the two sides face each other across a no-man's land. Tanks are described as an armored, all-terrain vehicle that can withstand small-arms fire and cross trenches. Wells foresaw huge, hundred-foot-long vehicles propelled by eight pairs of "pedrails," or wheels ringed with flexible feet to give traction. Their weapons were far ahead of their time: remotely controlled rifles with advanced sighting systems to allow for sharp accuracy while moving. Although he got the size wrong, in almost every other respect Wells accurately predicted the tanks that in 1917-1918 effectively ended World War I. And as *Popular Mechanics* foresaw in a 1915 feature "Gasoline Cavalry Displaces Horses," tanks returned battlefield maneuvering to warfare, taking soldiers out of the trenches and protecting them from rifle and machine gunfire.

But no one then envisioned that airplanes would become a dominant part of battles on the oceans, carried on ships far from land. Aircraft carriers were ideal targets, since they required deep decks and could not afford the weight of armoring the entire craft. As a result, penetrating bombs could gut an entire carrier in a single blow. A 1910 article extraordinarily anticipated the battle of Midway, which many cite as the most dramatic reversal of fortunes in naval warfare. There, the carrier surrounded by support ships became a queen bee at the center of her swarm. Kill the bee, kill the swarm. The Japanese navy never recovered from incisive attacks on their carriers, just half a year past the attacks on Pearl Harbor.

When machines dominate battle, maintenance and fuel become crucial. A 1933 *Popular Mechanics* piece noted, "Whoever in America can drive an automobile is already partially trained for service in the next war." A decade later, German divisions were astonished that Americans could fix their own tanks, jeeps, and even airplanes, just because they had grown up tinkering with the family car. German troops had no such experience. Culture can be as decisive as marksmanship.

Will the advantage always lie with the heavy tanks and massive aircraft carrier groups? Probably not. When engineers can put a TV camera and smart software into the nose of an armor-piercing bazooka round (or in Army lingo, "recoilless rifle"), tanks become prey. Add to the picture a soldier who can fiddle the joystick to make course corrections and the costly tank quickly becomes an endangered species. Economics bear this out: a single missile costs maybe a millionth of the tank's price.

The same might be eventually true of even aircraft carriers, if light robotic planes (or drones) can flit in just above the whitecaps and hammer through a hull. In warfare, evolution never sleeps. ◉

THE UNION OF SEA AND AIR

PREDICTION 1914 **Aviation and naval operations have become inextricably con-nected,** and the question of carrying flying boats along with a battle fleet, and even with individual ships, has become a problem of the most urgent kind. Two interesting solutions have recently been worked out. One of these is a ship built especially for the work of carrying flying boats, and the other is a biplane flying boat with wings that can be folded back along the sides of the body.

The ship will have a length of 354 feet and will be provided with flying decks both fore and aft. After much experiment, a biplane with hinged wings has been developed that is not only easily folded into a compact form for storage in a hangar or on the deck of a ship but is said to be safe and rigid when in flight. The span of the wings when extended is 70 feet from tip to tip of the upper plane, while the span of the lower plane is somewhat less. When the wings are folded back, the machine has an overall width of only 10 feet. In folding, it is only necessary to remove four pins and detach the stay wires from the floats, after which the wings are easily and quickly wound back. Each machine is equipped with slings and rings for lowering into the water and for raising aboard ship.

In the wars of the future, pursuit bombers will scout ahead and transmit information by radio to a force of heavy cruisers.

PREDICTION
1940

PREDICTION 1924 **Once believed by many to be a weapon of warfare** that would render big battleships obsolete, the airplane has been developed as an almost indispensable aid to naval units engaged in tactical maneuvering and long-distance firing. In addition to aerial mosquito fleets for bombing and torpedo attack, and to lay down effective smoke screens as an impediment to enemy offense, much attention has been paid to their value for scouting over the seas and as an aid to directing the fire of gunners who may be out of sight of their targets. While spotting the fall of the projectiles, the airmen observe and report all changes in the course and speed of moving enemy ships. On board the attacking craft, the range and elevation of the rifles are adjusted to conform with these data.

PREDICTION 1927 **Leading naval authorities hold that the development of aircraft,** which has been swift and startling, is not an indication that battleships are doomed, but that battleships, in conjunction with aircraft and utilizing the services that aircraft can perform, will become more and more deadly as weapons in future wars. To accomplish that union of sea and air, they have quietly been revolutionizing the surface ships while speeding the development of faster, bigger, and better-armed planes.

The aircraft carriers are the most weird and wonderful ships that ever put to sea. To get the maximum width of flying deck, they are built with an enormous flare, and all the superstructure, control rooms, smokestacks, wireless masts, and other accessories are placed far over to one side in order to leave the deck clear. Huge freight elevators lift the planes from the hangar deck below, bringing them up through great trapdoors, completely assembled and ready to fly. Below this deck is an airplane factory and machine shop, capable of rebuilding an entire plane or making any necessary repairs. Even the lifeboats and tenders have been moved from their davits and are carried slung in recesses along the side of the hull.

The future battleship may replace the present airplane catapults with an all-over flying deck armored with two or three inches of steel to resist thin-walled aerial bombs. Below it, the protective deck would be heavily armored, as at present, to stand off plunging shells and penetrating bombs. The turrets would be placed on this deck, firing from beneath the flying deck above.

PREDICTION 1931 **One British submarine is equipped to serve as mother ship for an amphibian airplane,** thus combining in one unit the eyes of the navy above and beneath the sea. The plane is packed inside the boat when it submerges and can be launched off the deck within six minutes after the vessel comes to the surface. The submarine contains a watertight hangar on the deck in which the plane rests when the boat submerges. The amphibian is equipped with folding wings in order to fit the hangar. On the deck of the vessel is a catapult from which the bird of war is launched at a speed of 50 miles per hour. When the submarine rises, the hangar is opened and the plane is moved onto the catapult, which is ready to operate as soon as the engine is started and the wings arc opened.

 PREDICTION 1951 **Before long the bow of a new behemoth, the likes of which the world has never seen, will cleave the seas.** What will the monolithic flattop aircraft carrier be like? Unfortunately, most of the fascinating facts about it are secure in Pentagon files, whose tightly locked drawers carry

PREDICTION 1931 A seaplane with folding wings is launched from a submarine via catapult, in this proposed setup.

STREAMLINED BATTLESHIP *OF THE FUTURE*

The war tests between battleship and bomber are leading to the streamlining of decks and turrets, not for aerodynamic reasons but to fend off aerial bombs, and the multiplication of anti-aircraft batteries. This whale-back battleship has a foredeck roofed with a heavy armor plate, quantities of anti-aircraft guns over the enclosed bridge, and a streamlined aft turret, below which is a hangar housing bombers, fighters, and reconnaissance planes launched by catapult.

How far television has been used in navies is another secret, but it has its place in the transmission of sketches, diagrams, and photographs inasmuch as these are often of vital importance but are non-communicable in words.

PREDICTION 1941 **A sensational innovation is the greatly improved motor torpedo boat.** In the War of 1914–1918 it was a fair-weather craft and threw a bow wave so conspicuous that it rendered a surprise attack next to impossible. Today's speedboats, however, are so light and highly powered that they skim over the water. Their two main engines are supplemented by a third small motor. This center engine can drive the boat at about nine knots, at which the bow wave is negligible and propeller noise so slight it cannot be picked up by enemy hydrophones. Thus the boat can creep up on one engine at night, fire its torpedoes, and escape at full speed with its main engines on.

WAGING WAR BENEATH THE WAVES

PREDICTION 1917 **When a submarine sinks, gets ensnared in a net, or for some reason becomes unmanageable while underwater,** there has to be some way for the crew to escape. The solution is a small auxiliary submarine that is normally held

PREDICTION 1943

NOISELESS SEA SKIMMER
FIGHTS SUBMARINES

Gliding swiftly over water, the sea skimmer, designed to fight submarines, does not transmit telltale noises through the water, since it is driven by an air propeller instead of a water screw. The sub-chaser can go nearly 50 miles per hour and is armed with a 20-mm. cannon, a machine gun, and four depth charges.

in a concave seat constructed in the top part of the large craft. In the event of an accident, members of the crew would enter the lifeboat, close the watertight hatchways, free the small craft by unscrewing two large bolts that anchor it to the larger one, and rise to the surface.

An artist's conception of a German U-boat darting through the water above a sunken merchantman — its recent prey.

PREDICTION
1943 **From Britain comes word of a radio "magic eye"** that enables an air or surface observer to spot a submarine when it comes to the surface to recharge its batteries, even on the darkest night. Bombing planes can search rapidly over a vast area of sea and, especially in smooth water, spot the underwater shadow of a submarine more readily than can a vessel on the surface. These depth charges, hurled from surface craft, and bombs, dropped from airplanes and blimps, are still the most effective anti-submarine weapons yet devised.

This cross-section of a proposed British submarine shows the deadly craft submerged, its periscopes just breaking the surface and leaving their telltale wake.

PREDICTION
1968

Far below the waves, a research station takes shape, guarded by a nuclear sub base and haunted by a sub-sea volcano.

PREDICTION 1945 We are too close to the sweat and blood of battle to understand the full significance of the great naval engagement of World War II, when the United States Navy defeated the Japanese Imperial Navy. The USS *Missouri* (pictured) played a key role in those maneuvers. There is no doubt, however, that history will rank it in importance with such decisive sea engagements as Trafalgar and Jutland. We predict that this great sea battle of October, 1944, Midway, will be one of the last full-scale naval battles to be fought in the Pacific for years to come.

PREDICTION 1948 **Future submarines powered by jet engines would be equipped with tubes to launch missiles containing atomic war heads.** The missile would be expelled from the tube to the surface of the water, where it instantly would release a launching platform from a compartment in the tail. When the missile is well on its course toward the target, the launching rockets would be jettisoned and wings would unfold from the side. A ramjet engine then would propel it to the target.

PREDICTION 1963 **New anti-submarine warfare (ASW) weapons and detection tools are constantly being devised.** One, a new kind of helicopter just now coming into the fleet, is designed for destroyer duty. Killer subs for tracking down undersea raiders are also becoming increasingly effective. Better sonar detection gear will permit the killers to pursue enemy subs into deep undersea valleys and thermal layers.

Nuclear-armed rockets, torpedoes, and depth charges have tremendously enlarged the lethal range of ASW weapons. An atomic torpedo can miss its target by a wide margin and still score a kill.

All this armament sounds impressive, but it is useless without detection equipment. According to a number of published reports, the navy is working on infrared heat-sensing equipment to zero in on a sub's warm-water wake; magnetic devices, operating from high-flying planes or earth satellites, that will trace a sub's movements; the Screamer, a magnetic radio device that will be strewn in narrow channels to lock onto a sub's hull; a transmitter that broadcasts a continuous signal to pinpoint the sub's movements; and the Sniffer, an airborne electronic instrument that detects submarines by sensing atomic changes in the air due to the exhaust from submarine engines. It can also detect the train of radioactive water behind nuclear subs.

PREDICTION 1968 **Within 10 years, it should be possible to assemble a scientific colony** thousands of feet below the surface atop the seamounts of the Mid-Atlantic Ridge. The U.S. Navy would play a major role in setting up such a research base. In an age when nuclear subs cruise submerged for months, undersea warfare experts have many ideas about military use of the seafloor. They're not talking about details, but it's apparent that taking the high ground will become as crucial as it is in land warfare. "If we can control the ridges, we can control the oceans," one weapons-oriented scientist said.

The navy has awarded several contracts to study designs for undersea stations rated at a depth of 6,000 feet. Perhaps such stations will be used as submarine bases (U.S. nuclear subs already cruise at 2,000 feet, according to best-educated guesses), communication centers, missile sites, or submarine-detection stations.

At such depths, scientists, though they explore submerged mountain ranges, must remain locked within their protective shells of steel or glass, traveling only by submarine or bottom crawler. Dependent on instruments for much of their perception, enabled by powerful lamps to see, they may well feel forever alien. (*See pages 124–125.*)

PREDICTION 1969 **New destroyers are joining the ASW fleet with sonar systems** powerful enough to bounce sound waves off the floor of the sea, thus extending their detection and tracking range. Some destroyers will have a new kind of sonar dome—made of rubber and pressurized—bulging under their hulls.

A new torpedo—more like an underwater guided missile—is adding uncanny accuracy to the firepower of these planes and ships. It carries a miniature sonar system so it can home in on a fleeing submarine and follow it through the wildest evasive maneuvers. If the torpedo strikes and misses, it automatically turns and strikes again!

Several new weapons are still in the planning stage or are being developed in secrecy. These include anti-submarine mines that would release homing torpedoes when triggered by the sound of an approaching sub. Other programs are even more speculative. Could sonobuoys like those now sending signals to aircraft be scattered over a wider area of the sea to be monitored by a satellite in orbit high above? Or could a satellite carry an infrared detector to trace the passage of a submerged nuclear sub by the heat from its reactor?

Conceivably, destroyers of the future might skim the surface of the sea on foils while their sonars on cables probe several hundred feet below. (*See pages 128–129.*)

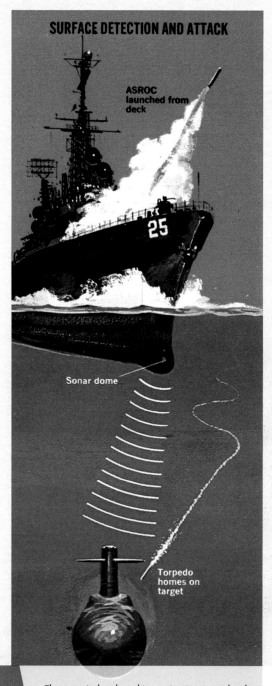

SURFACE DETECTION AND ATTACK

ASROC launched from deck

25

Sonar dome

Torpedo homes on target

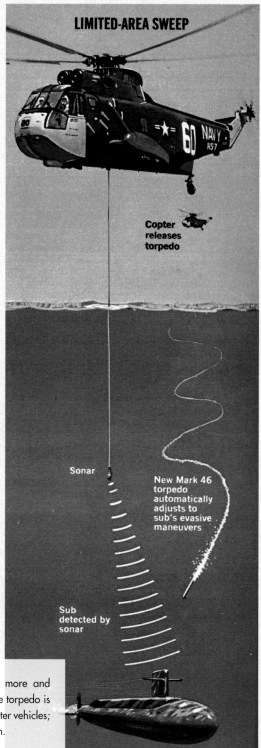

LIMITED-AREA SWEEP

60 NAVY HS-7

Copter releases torpedo

Sonar

New Mark 46 torpedo automatically adjusts to sub's evasive maneuvers

Sub detected by sonar

PREDICTION 1969

The navy's hard-working scientists are developing more and better ways of tracking and hunting submarines. One torpedo is designed to attain speeds now unheard of in underwater vehicles; the other tests a new nuclear-electric propulsion system.

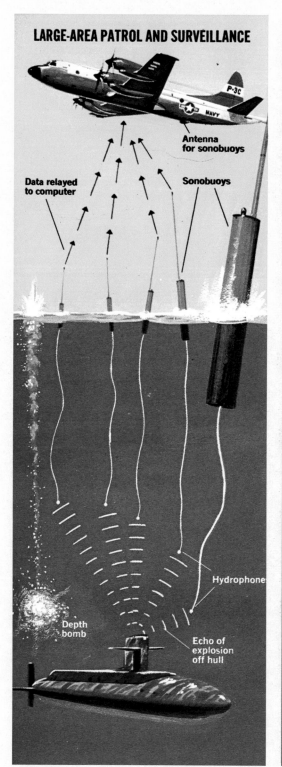

LARGE-AREA PATROL AND SURVEILLANCE

Antenna
for sonobuoys

Data relayed
to computer

Sonobuoys

Hydrophone

Depth
bomb

Echo of
explosion
off hull

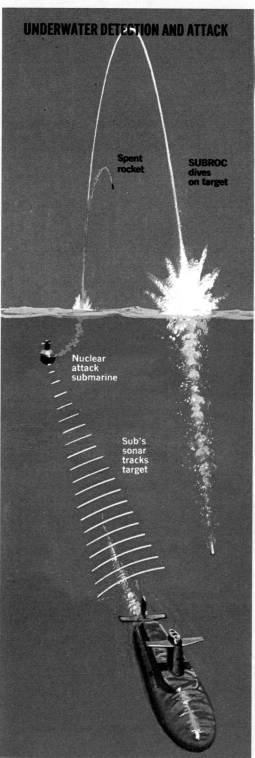

UNDERWATER DETECTION AND ATTACK

Spent
rocket

SUBROC
dives
on target

Nuclear
attack
submarine

Sub's
sonar
tracks
target

THE ARMY'S MOST FLEXIBLE WAR MACHINES

PREDICTION 1910 **The combined automobile and motorboat is not an entirely new idea,** but the first vehicle of the kind to be officially taken up by any government is the invention of a French engineer. The French war office believes it will prove of great service in scouting and in various other ways—for instance, for taking a line across a stream so that a temporary rope bridge may be fixed.

PREDICTION 1932 **Water offers no obstacles to an amphibian war tank** recently tested in England, which can swim across any river in its path. It is virtually a combined land and water battleship, for when in the water a steel turret containing small guns protrudes above the surface, so it can attack as it swims. A small propeller gives the tank a speed of about seven miles per hour in the water, while on land it can lumber over five-foot ditches with vertical banks, climb a steep grade at six miles per hour, or race across flat country at 40 miles.

The land-water tank was evolved after a satisfactory method was found for making elastic watertight joints. Several years ago, an amphibian tank was tried out, but it sank, due to the development of leaks in its non-elastic joints after rough cross-country travel.

PREDICTION 1940 **Inspired by achievements** of an amphibian tractor of his own invention, Donald Roebling has designed a monster land-and-water war tank, a working model of which is being built for the United States at a cost of $25,000. Plans call for a juggernaut capable of carrying forty soldiers and 7,000 pounds of equipment at

PREDICTION 1940 This drum-wheeled amphibian tank, adaptable to carrying heavy loads or bringing troops into battle, can travel over any ground and into the water as well.

LANDING SHIP OPENS TO REVEAL EAGER TROOPS

This landing ship can easily put armed, ready-to-fight Yanks and their equipment ashore. Afloat, the landing ship's nose trimly cleaves the water, giving scant hint of its double life. But once the craft has pushed up onto a hostile beach, the nose sections swing wide—they are in reality two huge, hinged doors. When they are open, a ramp inside is lowered. And over this ramp streams the complement of men and weapons.

25 miles per hour over land and 8.5 per hour on water. One possible use for the amphibian might be the transfer of troops from ships to the shore.

PREDICTION 1940 **Two Canadian inventors have just patented an amphibian tank designed to travel where no road exists**—over swamp, ice, water, and rugged hillside. An adaptation of the plan would make it a military fort. Its bargelike body, 35 feet long and 11 feet wide, would weigh about 20 tons and carry an 18-ton load; afloat, it would displace 12,000 cubic feet of water. Breaking from the two-rut tradition that dates from days of chariots, the plan calls for three gigantic wheels. Steering controls at both ends permit driving in either direction.

PREDICTION 1953 **Snow, mud, or water—it makes no difference to the Otter,** the amphibious cargo carrier that is now being built of aluminum to reduce its weight. Believed to be the first all-aluminum ground vehicle ever mass-produced, the Otter weighs only 4 tons. The army plans the vehicle for non-armored, non-combat use, and its weight fits it for airborne operations. It has a top speed of about 28 miles per hour on land and about 4 miles per hour in water when propeller-driven at the stern.

GASOLINE CAVALRY DISPLACES HORSES

PREDICTION 1914 **A completely armored train has been added to the fighting equipment of the French army.** This exemplar of modern war machinery is a powerful transportable fort designed for heavy fighting and able to withstand severe fire. It is composed of an armored locomotive, two heavily plated cars for the troops, and cars carrying rapid-fire guns mounted so that they may be swung to any point of the compass. On the car that follows immediately behind the engine is a conning tower where the officer directing the fire is positioned. The tops of the cars are fitted for the use of sharpshooters.

PREDICTION 1915 **Several European armies now engaged in war are using an American-made armored motorcar** designed to be driven from either end. It has four forward and reverse speeds, enabling it to be operated as rapidly in one direction as in the other and doing away with the necessity of having to turn the machine around before it can proceed in the opposite direction. The man at the front of the car has complete control of it when it is going forward, but when it is run backward, the steering wheel, brakes, and clutch are operated by the rear driver. The car is fitted with a central revolving turret, in which a machine gun is mounted. It can also be cranked from the driver's seat.

STEEL PUSH CARS FOR STORMING TRENCHES

The wheeled body shield is the latest scheme developed for protecting infantrymen during offensive operations against enemy trenches. It affords immunity from rifle bullets and shrapnel when advancing upon fortified positions. A long slit terminating in a porthole forms a lookout as well as a place through which to fire.

PREDICTION
1927 **The days when armored knights went forth to battle on steel-clad horses were revived recently** when the British army demonstrated its newest weapon, one-man tanks, to replace cavalry horses. Equipped with both caterpillar tread and rubber-tired wheels, either of which can be placed in operation at will, the little tanks are capable of making 30 miles per hour on smooth roads, can go any

wheel in the rear. When the wheels are raised and the caterpillar tread brought into action, the same handlebars do the steering in the same way that an ordinary caterpillar truck is managed.

PREDICTION 1943 **If the mammoth German tank** is not stopped during 1943, the United Nations will be forced into the competition for greater weight and more protective armor, and soon the tank is likely to take on the fearful proportions of a house. But if history does repeat itself, the monster-size tank will vanish from the face of the earth like the dinosaur, or like the steel-clad knight who ruled the Middle Ages but kept piling on defensive armor until it took a powerful horse to carry him into battle.

The function of the latest hit-and-run-type of tank buster is not to shuffle around trading heavy punches with a huge German tank, like two heavyweight palookas in a boxing ring. It takes a position, fires perhaps four or five rounds, speeds to another spot, hurls steel again, and then ducks once more, like a nimble boxer outpointing a slow slugger.

Conceivably, the tank could keep on growing until it gets too big for our railroad flat cars and too heavy for our highways, so that it will have to be shipped knocked down to battle areas and assembled there. This weapon is a challenge that must be answered, whatever its size.

PREDICTION 1942 This streamlined ammunition carrier, recently proposed to the U.S. Army by a Michigan designer, is well-armored and well-armed against attackers.

place a horse can be ridden, and get there much more quickly. In addition, the cavalryman on the gasoline-powered steed is completely sheltered behind bullet-proof steel.

On a road or over smooth ground, the baby tanks ride on three rubber-tired wheels and are steered by motorcycle-type handlebars, operating the single small

War tanks conquer all obstacles in war tests! Climbing over or smashing obstacles of the kind that may be experienced in actual warfare, army tanks demonstrated their effectiveness in the recent Austrian maneuvers at Bruck. Under conditions of modern warfare, these high speed "fortresses" might be expected to smash through barb-wire entanglements, leap narrow trenches, and perform numerous other duties as their crew mans guns from the interior.

PREDICTION
1937

5

TELEVISION EDUCATES

THE HOME GUARD

PREDICTION

1944

The war of the rockets burst into full flame with the invasion of Nazi Europe.

OUR ROBOT SPIES IN OUTER SPACE

PREDICTION 1957 **Man's inventiveness and curiosity will demand that larger and better-equipped satellites** be placed in orbit. These would be true satellites: they would orbit the earth at altitudes up to 1,000 miles, where lack of atmospheric drag would allow them to circle the earth for thousands of years.

PREDICTION 1957 **Future satellites may have instrumentation undreamed of today.** An era of satellites with radio powered by a nuclear power plant or solar batteries can be visualized in the foreseeable future. Such large satellites might carry television cameras aimed not only at the earth but at the skies, transmitting to permanent satellite observatories around the world a constant flow of cosmic information.

PREDICTION 1958 **Imagine this: orbiting at 16,000 miles per hour, a super-spy satellite swings high above the pole.** With each pass, it surveys yet another earth sector, thus keeping the whole world under daily surveillance.

As the satellite arcs toward enemy territory, a half dozen camera ports slide open. Solar-powered, an image orthicon—akin to a television's picture tube—comes suddenly alive. Radar reaches through miles of atmosphere and murk. Moments later, through a hole in the overcast, the orthicon tube's flat face unmasks an airfield and the fuzzy yet discernible outlines of its hundred atomic bombers. Farther on, the infrared detectors strip a steel mill bare of camouflage, as the telltale heat from its blast furnace burns indelibly into the detectors' filmstrip memories.

Forty-five minutes later, the satellite orbits over friendly territory. Once more its timer clicks, energizing powerful transmitters. Far below, complex recorders receive the intelligence report not even one hour old.

"Film," explains one researcher, "will have only limited application in the spy-satellite camera. For once exposed and developed, the negative is dead weight and useless." We whimsically can anticipate the manned satellite by imaging ourselves in the 21-inch sphere during its initial revolutions. The end of such an imaginary trip would be little less spectacular than the beginning. After a few months to a year, the resistance of even rare atmosphere would exert a toll. Slowly its orbit would shrink, carrying it closer to Earth. At this stage, you'd better get off—preferably with an asbestos parachute.

SETTING TRAPS FOR ENEMY SHIPS

PREDICTION 1914 A bomb hangs from captive balloons, mining the clouds to protect a camp or fortress against aerial attack. The line on which the bomb is suspended is attached to the trigger. The weight of the apparatus is not sufficient to trip this, but the slightest additional weight—or a jerk— would instantaneously cause an explosion. A flying machine approaching unseen during the night might be blown to pieces merely by striking one of the wires that are completely invisible in the darkness.

PREDICTION 1964 If the Russians have won the race for an anti-missile missile, as they have been hinting lately with the AM-1 installation, it would give them a massive advantage in any nuclear war. But Pentagon officials say that Russia has far from won the race. They compare the Russian anti-missile system with a U.S. weapons system that is not considered effective enough to put into production—the Army's bug-ridden Nike-Zeus. It's now considered only an experimental system that will lead to a more sophisticated weapon, the Nike-X.

 PREDICTION 1958 Soon satellites will observe, capture, and transmit photos of every moment on every spot on earth.

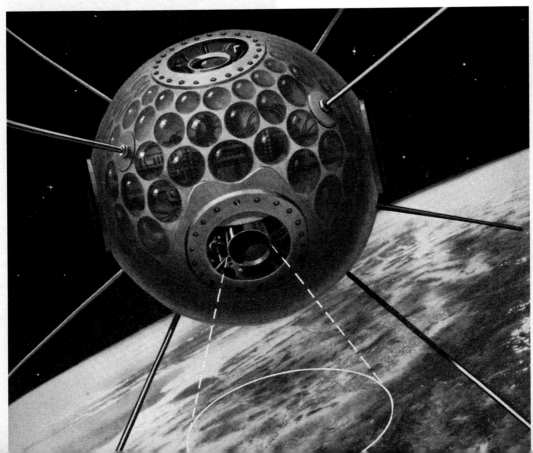

PREDICTION
1939

Aerial minefields guard against airplane raids. Small bombs are suspended by wires from hydrogen-filled balloons. It is claimed that the balloons can be regulated to float at the altitude desired.

A Nike-Zeus battery can take on eight or nine warheads at the same time. But it can't stop dozens of missiles swarming from several directions, each warhead spewing out a cluster of realistic decoys in addition to the live payload.

U.S. officials believe the AM-1 at Leningrad is largely a propaganda maneuver, meant to reassure Russia's satellite countries and impress neutral nations. The Pentagon also believes that AM-1 is a test system for developing a mobile

PREDICTION

1941

A REAL AERIAL *DEFENSE LINE*

SYNCHRONIZED MACHINE GUN SHOOTS THROUGH ROTOR BLADES

SYNCHRONIZED MACHINE GUN SHOOTS THROUGH PROPELLER

ROTATING MACHINE GUN

A fleet of super-gyros such as the one depicted here, heavily moored to stand off raiding planes, are predicted to hover over an area the army wants to protect, ready to meet dive bombers or any other attacking aircraft with a deadly barrage of firepower.

missile defense to accompany armies in the field.

Who, then, is really winning the anti-missile missile race? The Defense Department, and many outside scientists, say neither side is winning. Many experts think there will never be a successful anti-missile missile.

PREDICTION 1911 A French artist's idea of how coast defenses will appear in the future, fitted with powerful searchlights and huge guns to repel attacks by aerial craft.

PROTECTION FROM THE CLOUDS OF DEATH

PREDICTION 1921 **An outgrowth of the rehabilitation measures** adopted by France in the reclaiming of her poison-gas-wrecked veterans, is an inhalation treatment claimed to be beneficial in afflictions of the lungs and air passages, such as bronchitis and tuberculosis. The healing gases are generated in large retorts and, after passing through washing and filtering chambers, are delivered to inhaler mouthpieces under

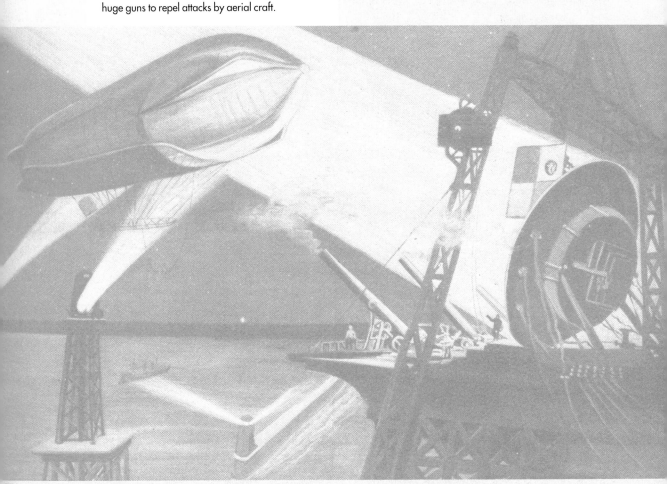

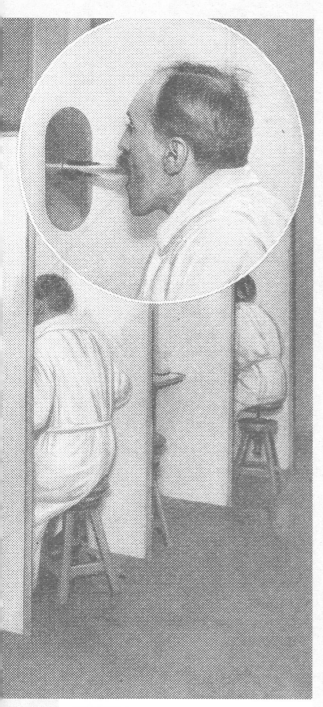

pressure. From these the patients inhale certain dosages at prescribed times. The generating plant is quite elaborate, as is also the piping system, so that the whole is housed in a special institution called an "inhalatorium." The patients reside at the institution, where they are kept under constant supervision and observation. The original installation is under the charge of the Ministry of War, but it is safe to predict that, if the treatment proves as effective as it is hoped it may, other institutions will be built for the benefit of the public.

PREDICTION 1921 In a new mask perfected by the Navy Bureau of Ordnance, the use of a mouthpiece, which was such an objectionable feature to the wearer of the old masks, has been eliminated. The clumsy bag that was used in the old masks for carrying the chemical tank, and which, hanging on the wearer's chest, was in many ways an encumbrance, has been dispensed with. The chemical tank now forms part of the mask itself and is carried on the head. Short feed-pipes lead from it to two openings just above the eyes. The canister has been greatly improved and strengthened.

For naval use it has the particular advantage of being specially adapted to safeguard the crews of submarines from the danger that so frequently occurs in underwater work due to the formation of carbon monoxide, one of the most deadly gases in existence.

PREDICTION 1925 An all-purpose mask developed by army chemists is equally useful in mines, factories, battlefields, and laboratories, since its canister holds protection against all known poison gases.

PREDICTION 1925 **Although the use of poison gas in warfare may be outlawed,** the U.S. Army will be prepared to protect its carrier pigeons, horses, mules, dogs, and other animals from the fumes should occasion arise, for special masks have been devised to shield beasts and birds in the service. The protector for horses and mules consists of a cheesecloth bag that covers the nostrils and upper jaw only—because they breathe only through the nose, it is not necessary to cover the mouth. Their eyes need no protection against teargas for they have no tear ducts. The dog mask is similar, but covers both the upper and lower jaws. The pigeons will wear no

PREDICTION 1917

PREDICTION 1925

PREDICTION 1934

The evolution of gas masks for military animals.

protectors while in flight, but will be guarded from gas by a special shield entirely covering their transport cages.

PREDICTION 1934 **Preparation for safety in time of war is being taught by several European governments.** The latest device for preserving human life against the effects of poison gas is an artificial respirator exhibited by the Belgian Civil Union. The respirator is intended for treating civilians and soldiers stricken by gas that an enemy air squadron might release over a city. Its use, for the present, is confined to one victim at the time.

PREDICTION 1943 **Training of the army in gas defense is a tremendous task.** One of the big dangers in gas attack is the psychological response of untrained personnel. Because gas is a particularly frightening weapon, the men must be trained patiently and thoroughly so that their instinctive fears may be overcome. The first step is to teach them that their masks will provide adequate protection. First, they are required to enter a room filled with teargas while wearing the masks; then, at a signal, they remove the masks, give their names and army serial numbers, and rush for the door and fresh air, many of them with tears streaming down their faces.

GLASS CASE PROTECTS BABY

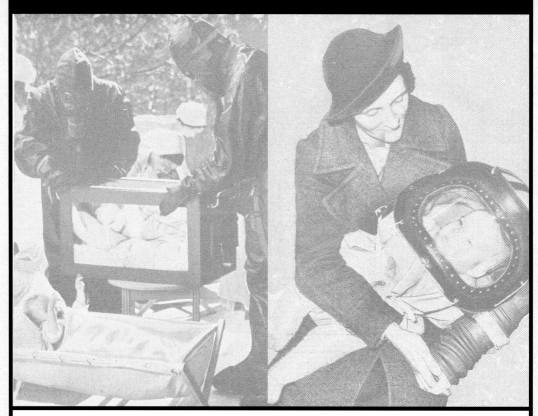

The latest invention of war-fearing Europe is a portable glass case into which babies can be thrust at the alarm of a gas attack and carried to a zone of safety. Another option, designed for infants up to two years of age, is a helmet that covers the entire upper portion of the body and straps closely about the waist. A constant supply of fresh air is pumped into the chamber by a hand-operated bellows.

PREDICTION **1943** **Any closed-type vehicle can be converted into a ventilated, gas-proof shelter** by an installation devised by Lieutenant Colonel Alvin Caldwell of the Chemical Warfare Service. This consists of filters installed beneath the hood of the vehicle—what Lieutenant Colonel Caldwell terms an "auto gas mask." The equipment can easily be installed by the average car owner. Once it was in place, the owner would have a ready-made shelter at hand, in the event the enemy should attempt gas raids on civilians.

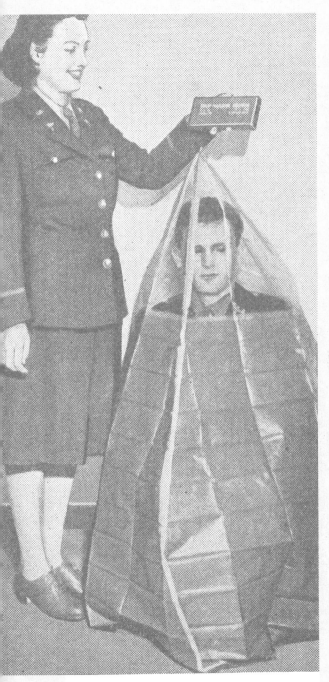

AVERTING DOOM FROM THE SKIES

PREDICTION 1927 **Soviet officials in Moscow are busy at work planning a gas- and bomb-proof city** capable of resisting attack from the air. The plans call for vast subterranean cities covered by reinforced-concrete roofs, which in turn are buried under many feet of sod and earth. Railways and streets, as well as sidewalks, would also be placed underground.

Those buildings permitted above ground would be limited to four stories. The outer walls would taper to offer the smallest possible target from above, and they would be surmounted by triple reinforced-concrete roofs, with honeycomb air spaces between to take up the shock of an exploding bomb. Not all bombs explode on contact, but the triple roofs would offer sufficient resistance to stop even a penetration-type bomb and explode it before the interior of the building could be reached.

Every outlet to the air, including all doors and windows, would be rendered gas-proof, while the underground passages and refuge rooms would be protected against poison gas by double doors, elaborate ventilating systems, and powerful exhaust fans, which could sweep a strong current of air across all openings to form an invisible barrier that would brush gas fumes away. Another idea advanced by the Russians is the building of powerful gas

PREDICTION 1943 U.S. military experts have devised an individual protective covering that unfolds from pocket-size and repels liquid gas.

neutralizers, which would draw the gas-laden air through water spray and chemicals and re-release it as pure air.

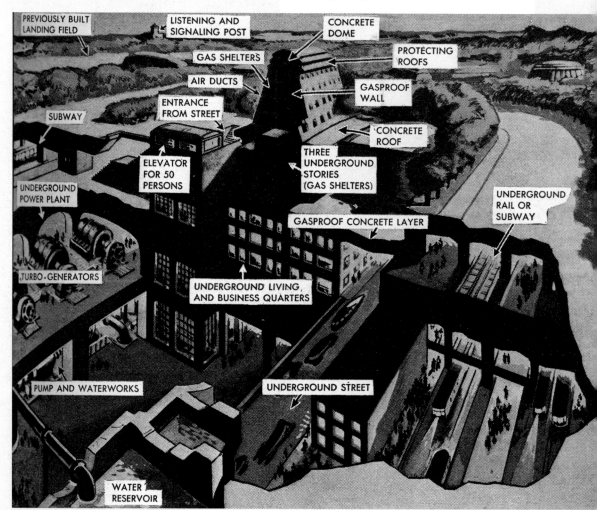 **PREDICTION 1941 The employment of common sand could convert miles of New York City's thinly roofed subways into air-raid shelters** for 3.5 million persons. It seems that sand has the same properties as anyone's lazy relative: As long as it is supported, it is no stronger than the support. But if the

support is removed, the sand packs down, forms an arch, and supports itself.

Sand is shoveled onto a thin, bending corrugated metal sheet, which keeps it from sifting through. The area above the metal sheet has been divided for about one

PREDICTION 1941 A proposed design for an "underground skyscraper" which would shield citizens and structures from bombing and gas.

PREVIOUSLY BUILT
LANDING FIELD

LISTENING AND
SIGNALING POST

CONCRETE
DOME

PROTECTING
ROOFS

GAS SHELTERS

AIR DUCTS

GASPROOF
WALL

ENTRANCE
FROM STREET

SUBWAY

CONCRETE
ROOF

ELEVATOR
FOR 50
PERSONS

THREE
UNDERGROUND
STORIES
(GAS SHELTERS)

UNDERGROUND
POWER PLANT

UNDERGROUND
RAIL OR
SUBWAY

GASPROOF CONCRETE LAYER

TURBO-GENERATORS

UNDERGROUND LIVING
AND BUSINESS QUARTERS

PUMP AND WATERWORKS

UNDERGROUND STREET

WATER
RESERVOIR

HANGAR UNDER PALISADES SEEN AS BOMB SHELTER

Huge bombproof tunnels dug out of the rocky Palisades on the Hudson River are visualized as a possibility by George J. Atwell, who heads a construction company. He proposes a tunnel consisting of a number of chambers serving as air-raid shelters, hospitals, and airplane hangars that would be able to withstand the pounding of heavy bombs.

foot by vertical walls of ordinary fly screen and an occasional I-beam. Above this, horizontal walls of the same fly screen divide the sand into layers for four or five feet—whereupon the sand produces a remarkable phenomenon. Laboratory experiments have shown that such a slab of loose sand and fly screen can resist a vertical load of more than 3,000 pounds per square foot and is more valuable in resisting concussion than a foot of reinforced concrete.

It happens that many subway stations have an intermediate, or mezzanine, floor between the platforms below and the streets above. Installing rows of 14-inch I-beams, laying strips of corrugated metal, soldering in fly screen, and shoveling sand into the mezzanine of compartments promises to be a cheap method of saving thousands of lives if the need arises.

 PREDICTION 1953 Radioactive contaminants will be washed off by this clever underwater entrance to a bomb-proof sanctuary. (*See on page 158.*)

YOUR PREFAB BOMB-PROOF HOME

PREDICTION 1929 **To protect homes from poison-gas raids during a war,** a French expert has suggested a plan for covering houses by a shield of water, released from pipes on the roof. The blanket, he asserts, would neutralize the effects of the gas and so spare the occupants of the buildings.

POOL

PREDICTION 1941 At the Newark College of Engineering, Professor Albert has designed what he calls the "Bompus-Rumpus Room" because it is a place where "bombs won't raise a rumpus." He suggests that every new home be equipped with such underground rooms. This bombproof cellar might be divided into three parts: one for living, one for sleeping, and the third as a utility room.

PREDICTION 1941 In a recent demonstration of precast concrete houses and backyard "tepee" bomb shelters, the walls, partitions, and roof of a three-room house were erected in just 23 minutes. Its walls would stop all but the heaviest flying fragments, the house was designed for quick construction for defense industry workers. The walls, floors, and roof panels are precast in forms flat on the ground and are made of an aggregate which is 60 percent pumice.

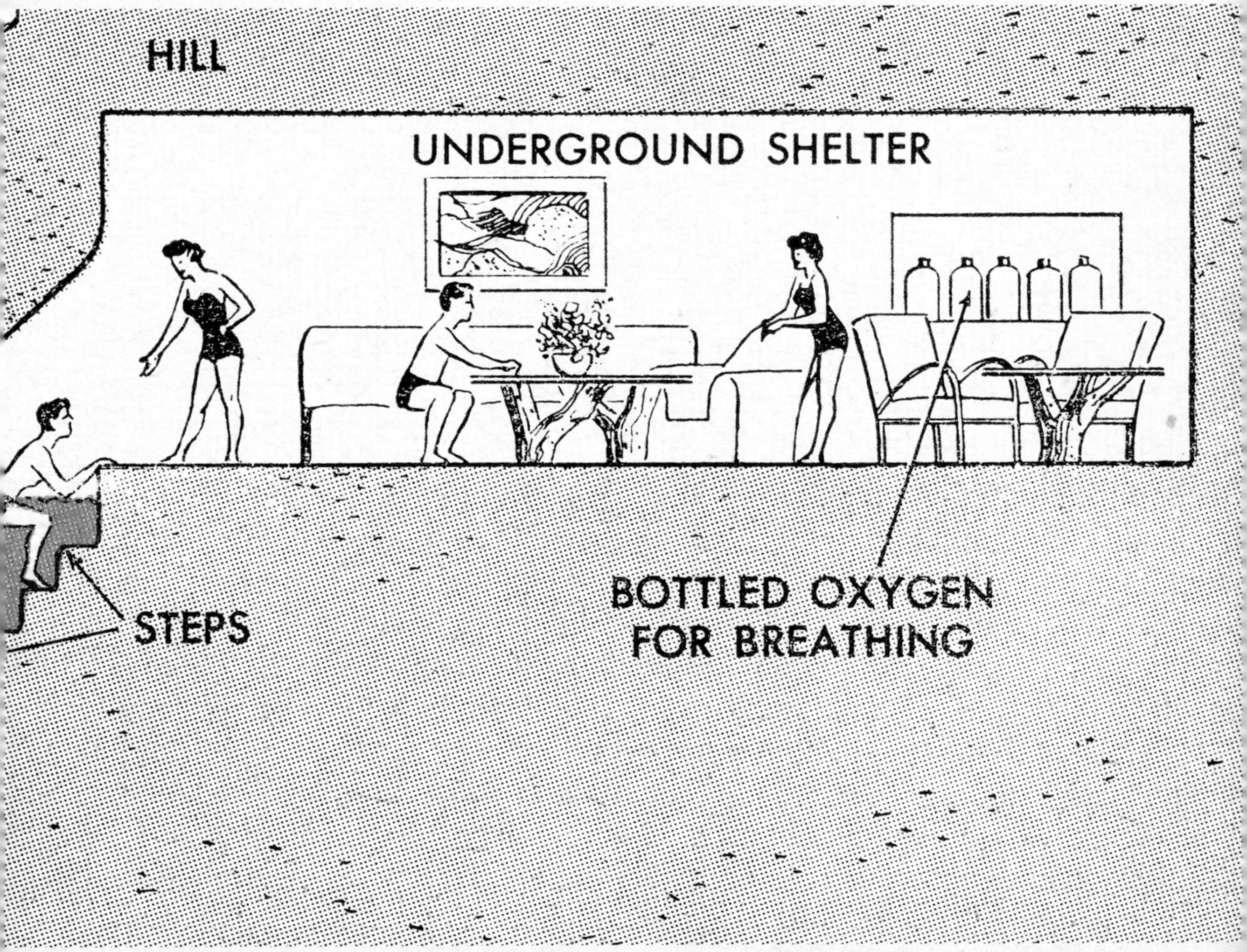

HILL

UNDERGROUND SHELTER

STEPS

BOTTLED OXYGEN FOR BREATHING

LUXURY SHELTER KEEPS YOU SAFE IN STYLE

California architect and interior designer Paul László has designed a deluxe bomb shelter in Los Angeles that provides quarters for eight persons for two weeks. Comfortably supplied with food, water, electricity, and filtered air, the shelter's occupants would be in touch with the world by shortwave radio. A Geiger counter with a protected tube located aboveground would tell the occupants when surface contamination had been reduced to a safe level.

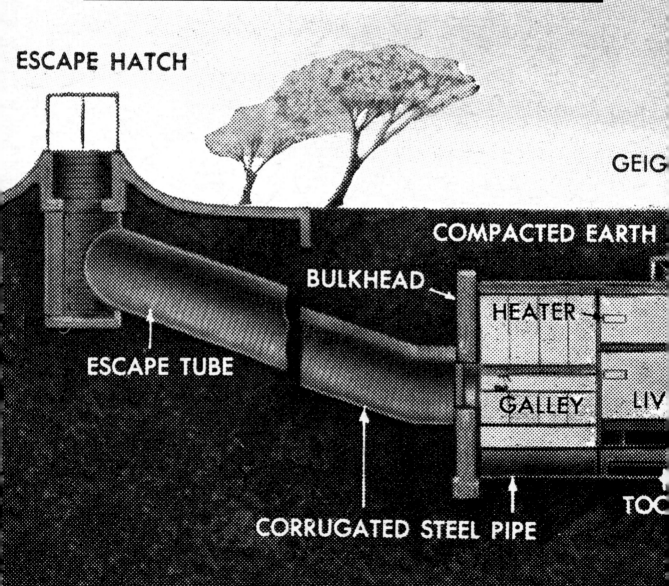

ESCAPE HATCH

GEIG

COMPACTED EARTH

BULKHEAD

HEATER

ESCAPE TUBE

GALLEY

LIV

CORRUGATED STEEL PIPE

TOO

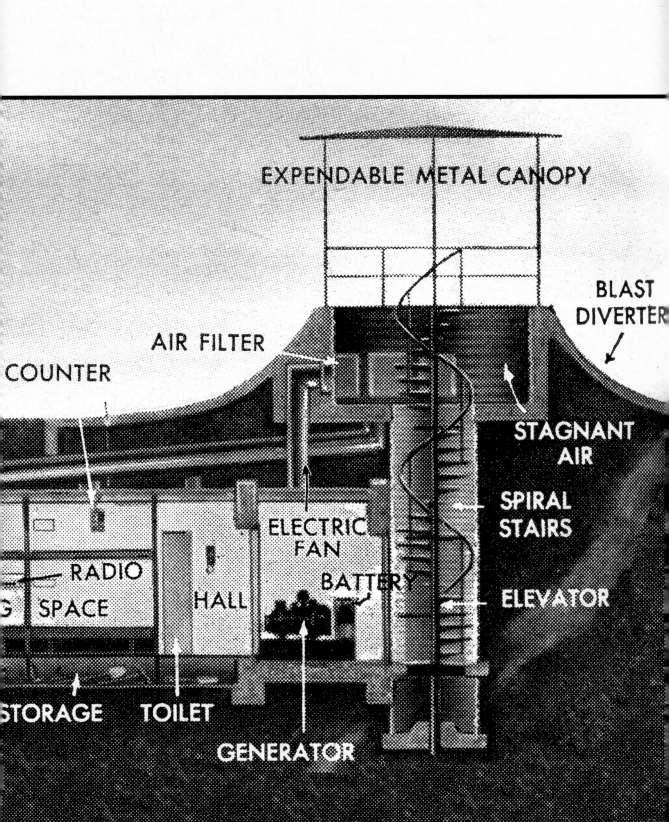

EXPENDABLE METAL CANOPY

BLAST DIVERTER

AIR FILTER

COUNTER

STAGNANT AIR

SPIRAL STAIRS

ELECTRIC FAN

RADIO SPACE

BATTERY

HALL

ELEVATOR

STORAGE

TOILET

GENERATOR

PREDICTION 1951 **Atom-bomb shelters are now available in prefabricated form.** The parts are shipped by flatbed trailer, unloaded at the purchaser's home, and lowered into a backyard excavation. The entrance section of the shelter has a steel lid, a slide down the center for fast entrance, and stairs at the side. It fits into an opening cast in the main section. Still another section is a vertical escape hatch equipped with ladder rungs and a steel lid. This hatch is connected to the shelter by standard sewer tile and may be installed at any desired distance away.

PREDICTION 1953 **A swimming pool that becomes an automatic decontamination bath** during an A-bomb attack is one of the features of a home that Hal B. Hayes, Hollywood contractor, is completing for himself. In the hillside next to the swimming pool, he's building an underground sanctuary reached by diving into the pool. His house is designed to "bring the outdoors indoors" for ordinary peaceful living, yet has a structure built to resist great destructive forces.

A continuation of his living room rug is pulled up to shroud the glass wall in that room when a button is pressed. Other walls of the house have a fluted design to resist shock wave and a fireproof exterior surface of Gunite. A garden growing in half a foot of soil on the flat roof provides insulation against extreme heat or shock. All exposed

Today's joyriders and skeet shooters could be tomorrow's soldiers. Driving experience is a boon to the Army man.

PREDICTION
1947

wood, inside and outside the house, is fire-resistant redwood coated with fire-retardant paint. In addition to the underground sanctuary, equipped with bottled oxygen, there is a bombproof shelter in the house itself, consisting of a large steel-and-concrete vault containing a sitting room and bathroom. Other features of the home include a three-story indoor tree.

TRAINING THE ARMY BEHIND THE ARMY

PREDICTION 1933 The mechanized cavalry regiment will far exceed the old mounted regiment in efficiency and in fighting force. It is capable of greater endurance and far greater marching power. If our first regiment of mechanized cavalry proves the success its sponsors anticipate, it is not too much to say that nearly all of our mounted regiments will be reorganized—without horses. And our first regiment of "motorized field artillery" has now been underway sufficiently long to promise great success.

This means that whoever in America can drive an automobile is already partially trained for service in the next war. A young man who gaily drives his automobile on some peaceful errand, at 60 miles or more per hour, is better equipped to become an effective member of a modern army than one of those rough-riding cowboys who hastened to join up in 1898.

PREDICTION 1940 Today's fighting pilot has to be an expert *and* a scientist because he is either flying a meteor or a monster, a fighting plane that streaks along at 300 to 400 miles per hour or a huge bomber like our flying fortresses. A man must have at least 750 hours of flight training before he is qualified to begin on bombers, and it takes one year to produce a pursuit pilot.

In Germany, every youngster starts his study of aviation at the age of ten. In America, a few months ago, only 500 out of 20,000 high schools had any aviation activities. Let's teach aviation in our schools and in our everyday life. Let's carry by air all first-class mail dispatched distances of 100 miles or more. Let's use the vast facilities already built up in our commercial airlines to make us into an air-conscious and air-skilled people. Let's use these strategic factors that no other nation in the world can equal to develop more airplanes, more pilots, and more maintenance personnel.

Consider what this one step would do. At no cost to the government, our peacetime aviation industry would be increased 200 times—not 200 percent, but 200 times! This policy would make peaceful aviation a mass industry that would absorb millions of young men eager to get into it. This program would create work for a peacetime air "army," but an "army" nevertheless so formidable in numbers and so experienced in the air that it would give any enemy pause.

PREDICTION 1942 **Regardless of the efficiency of the trained forces, civilians must take a hand in their own defense.** The time may come when every able-bodied American citizen, male and female, will be required to assume some protective duty in the army behind the army.

What may be in store for the average American as the civilian defense program expands is indicated by the intensive advanced training given volunteer auxiliary firemen in New York. To ordinary firefighting, first aid, morale building, house wrecking, and rescue work were added new problems inflicted by war hazards.

PREDICTION 1935 Student nurses are trained in the use of gas masks for protection during wartime attack. In the future, many wartime tasks will fall to civilians.

6

ATOMIC POWER
FOR PEACE

Optimism abounded at the dawn of the 20th century. From steam to harnessing the power of the atom, this was the era of power, starting with the internal combustion engine. A 1919 *Popular Mechanics* article glimpsed the future when it discussed the "possibility of the adoption of internal combustion engines for the propulsion of battleships." Engines not much different from those first developed in cars quickly dominated naval warfare. But the largest advance came with the adoption of diesel engines (also known as a compression-ignition engine). The engine was developed by Rudolf Diesel in 1893 and took over naval warfare, and later, land warfare by their adoption into tanks.

Desire for speed ramped up, a necessity for the military doctrine dryly called "mass and maneuver." As the Confederate general Nathan Bedford Forrest famously said, "I got there first with the most men," often quoted as "Get there firstest with the mostest." In the 1930s, liquid hydrogen was the so-called fuel of the future, expected to revolutionize air transport. Aircraft engineers like Igor Sikorsky claimed "an airplane using liquid hydrogen could circumnavigate earth along the equator in a non-stop flight without refueling." Today, this is eerily prescient, for liquid hydrogen plus liquid oxygen is now the dominant fuel for our powerful rockets. But it doesn't work in

Jet "donkeys" will give bigger jets a boost to help them launch from very short runways.

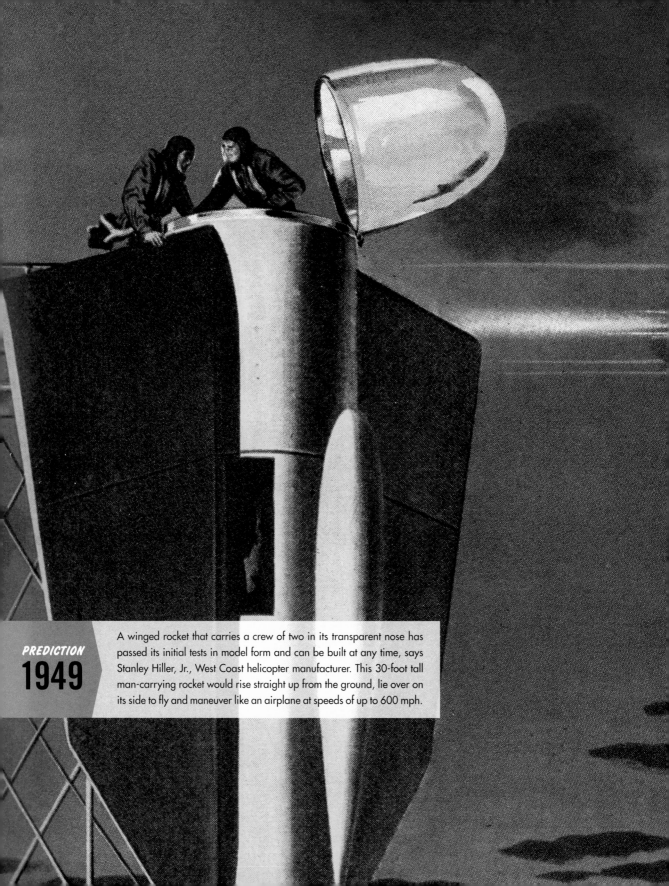

A winged rocket that carries a crew of two in its transparent nose has passed its initial tests in model form and can be built at any time, says Stanley Hiller, Jr., West Coast helicopter manufacturer. This 30-foot tall man-carrying rocket would rise straight up from the ground, lie over on its side to fly and maneuver like an airplane at speeds of up to 600 mph.

airplanes because at such high speeds, it becomes difficult to control their flight.

Speculation sometimes got out of hand. In 1941 the magazine thought that the plane of the future might get its power from several different sources, from the sun to magnets to combinations of yet discovered airplanes. Few of these ideas, however remarkable, penciled out. (A notable exception being the solar plane.) But other technologies did.

Incorporating electronic communication within a battleship allowed for far quicker action than old style battleships, which required orders to be shouted down sound pipes. The *Titanic* was the first civilian vessel assisted via radio signals, and its lesson was not lost on the navies.

But by the end of World War II, everyone was caught up in the power of the atom. The nuclear reactor seemed capable of anything, and indeed, did change naval war. Today dozens of battleships powered by nuclear reactors sail the seas, mostly United States vessels.

However, some predictions were bizarrely shortsighted. A 1938 prediction that airplanes could draw power from energy beamed to them had no concept of the huge energy costs of flight. Beaming that much power would make an antenna melt unless it was a kilometer wide. It's always a good idea to do a sanity check before peering into the crystal ball, but sometimes, it's okay to dream. ◎

NAVAL EXPERTS HERALD THE MOTOR-DRIVEN WARSHIP

PREDICTION 1906 **The reciprocating steam engine has, until recently, been used universally as a prime mover for large installations.** The advent—and rapid development—of large internal combustion engines during the last two or three years has altered the situation, and now a number of installations in which internal combustion engines have been used are now in satisfactory operation. Except for rare cases, the internal combustion engine will eventually entirely supersede the steam engine.

PREDICTION 1910 **Naval experts all over the world are eagerly awaiting the result of** the action of the British admiralty in ordering internal combustion engines for one of its new unarmored cruisers.

Percival A. Ilislam, in the *London Graphic*, writes: "What a marvelous half-century of naval development this will appear when its full history comes to be written! Iron displaced wood, and steel has succeeded iron. Sails and spars have disappeared, ousted by the steam engine; and when the steam engine reaches perfection in the turbine, it, in turn, finds itself challenged by internal combustion. Muzzle-loading guns have gone;

KEY

1 & **2** Admiral's Quarters

3 Aeroplanes

4 – **9** Warrant Officers' Quarters and Lifeboats

10 Wireless Operator's Room

11 Chart Room

12 Petty Officers' Quarters

13 Drill Deck

This diagram reveals the secrets of the motor-driven battleship of the future.

OIL TANK

OIL TANK

14 & **15** Officers' Quarters and Ward Room

16 & **17** Hospital

18 – **21** Crew's Quarters

22 Submarine

23 Stern Torpedo Room

24 Armory

25 – **27** Ammunition

28 Provisions

29 Ammunition

30 Dynamos

31 Forward Torpedo Room

32 Storeroom

33 Dynamos

34 Ammunition

35 & **36** Gas Engines

37 & **38** Ammunition

39 & **40** Mines

41 Torpedo Stores

42 Boatswain's Stores

43 Carpenter

44 & **45** Provisions

46 Conning Tower

PREDICTION 1909 The steamless, smokeless battleship, with no funnels to offer fine targets to the enemy, marks the next step in naval construction.

torpedoes, submarines, airships and wireless telegraphy have come. How long, we wonder, will it be before electricity throws the whole of our latest developments into the limbo of the obsolete?"

PREDICTION 1931 **The commanding officer of an electric battleship can get quicker action** than the commanding officer of an old-style battleship. Some 50,000 miles of wires carry electricity around the *West Virginia*, and through them the commanding officer not only can make his commands heard but motors can shift the propellers from full speed ahead to full speed astern in

six seconds. Of course the forward motion of the great ship itself takes more than mere moments to reverse, but the propellers will be churning great quantities of water in the opposite direction in less time than you take to read this sentence.

Besides propelling these modern steel dogs of war, electricity also helps point the guns, fire them, and enables the dreadnaughts to fire over the horizon at an enemy not even the lookout in the fighting top can see. Radio, crackling through the

GIANT *SUBATOMIC* SUBMARINE TANKER

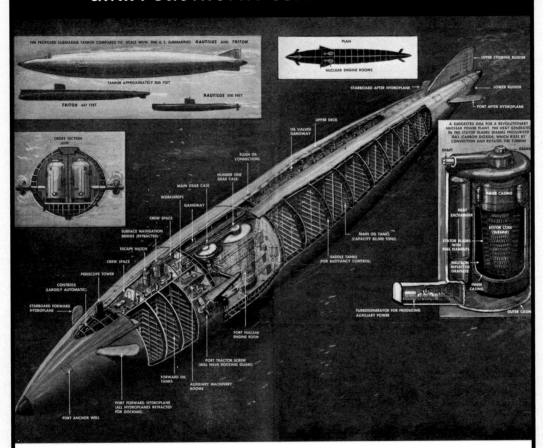

THE PROPOSED SUBMARINE TANKER COMPARED TO SCALE WITH THE U. S. SUBMARINES *NAUTILUS* AND *TRITON*

TANKER APPROXIMATELY 800 FEET

NAUTILUS 300 FEET

TRITON 447 FEET

PLAN

NUCLEAR ENGINE ROOMS

UPPER STEERING RUDDER

STARBOARD AFTER HYDROPLANE

LOWER RUDDER

PORT AFTER HYDROPLANE

CROSS SECTION

UPPER DECK

OIL VALVES GANGWAY

A SUGGESTED IDEA FOR A REVOLUTIONARY NUCLEAR POWER PLANT. THE HEAT GENERATED IN THE STATOR BLADES WARMS PRESSURIZED GAS (CARBON DIOXIDE) WHICH RISES BY CONVECTION AND ROTATES THE TURBINE

SHAFT

GEARS

FLUSH OIL CONNECTIONS

NUMBER ONE GEAR CASE

MAIN GEAR CASE

WORKSHOPS

GANGWAY

CREW SPACE

SURFACE NAVIGATION BRIDGE (RETRACTED)

ESCAPE HATCH

CREW SPACE

PERISCOPE TOWER

CONTROLS (LARGELY AUTOMATIC)

STARBOARD FORWARD HYDROPLANE

INNER CASING

HEAT EXCHANGER

ROTOR CORE (TURBINE)

STATOR BLADES WITH FUEL ELEMENTS

NEUTRON REFLECTOR GRAPHITE

INNER CASING

MAIN OIL TANKS (CAPACITY 80,000 TONS)

SADDLE TANKS (FOR BUOYANCY CONTROL)

CONTROLS

TURBOGENERATOR FOR PRODUCING AUXILIARY POWER

OUTER CASING

PORT NUCLEAR ENGINE ROOM

PORT TRACTOR SCREW (WILL HAVE DOCKING GUARD)

FORWARD OIL TANKS

AUXILIARY MACHINERY ROOMS

PORT FORWARD HYDROPLANE (ALL HYDROPLANES RETRACTED FOR DOCKING)

PORT ANCHOR WELL

This submarine tanker tests a new type of nuclear power plant. Power may be produced directly by incorporating fuel elements in the fixed blades of a turbine engine. Heat from the blades would cause pressurized gas to rise by convection, rotating the turbine. It is believed the power plant could drive the tanker at the great speed of 40 to 50 knots. A crew of about twelve men would be sufficient, as many of the controls would be automatic.

air from observation planes catapulted from the ship deck, enables gun crews to swing the muzzles of those giant weapons and send armor-piercing shells out beyond the "bend in the ocean."

There have been all manner of predictions and suggestions for the use of a thermoelectric engine. Speaking of this development before Congress last year, Admiral A. M. Morgan said, "We are on the verge of a breakthrough that will enable us to get efficiencies comparable to conventional power plants. In submarines, it would eliminate almost all noisy machinery. We should have something definite on this in three years." Wernher von Braun has suggested the use of these generators, operated by the heat of the sun, to provide power for space satellites; Dr. Wilson has drawn up plans for a similar device. And last year, at a meeting of the Institute of Radio Engineers, it was remarked that a silent thermoelectric lawnmower would be a boon to suburbia.

SUN-POWERED PLANES CIRCLE THE GLOBE

PREDICTION 1933 **One of the British air squadrons is using gasoline made from coal in its planes.** The gasoline is a by-product of an industry making a smokeless fuel and is said to be cheaper than the oil from coal produced by a hydrogenation process. It is claimed this fuel has the highest anti-knock values of any on the British market, that it requires no additional chemicals, and has a negligible gum content.

PREDICTION 1938 **When someone develops a safe, economical method of producing and handling liquid hydrogen,** he will probably revolutionize air transport. Igor Sikorsky, aircraft engineer, says an air-

PREDICTION 1957

ATOMIC BOMBER CARRIES FIGHTER ESCORT

A nuclear-powered bomber could travel to its target at high subsonic speeds. If alerted by its own radar to imminent enemy attack, it would then cut loose its escort of supersonic fighters, who would escort the mother ship through heavily defended areas. A comparatively small crew working in shifts could man the tow plane while amply shielded from radiation.

plane using liquid hydrogen could circumnavigate the planet along the equator in a non-stop flight without refueling.

PREDICTION 1941 **Civilization has stood aghast at the role the airplane has played** in altering the map of the world and changing the skylines of bombed cities scattered all the way from Europe to the Orient. Before many years, when the world has had a chance to bind its war wounds and turn its attention to the improvement of what is left of civilization, the impact of the airplane on other forms of transportation is likely to be as awe-inspiring as those first mass-bombing attacks on the great city of London.

During the various stages of progress, the motive power of the plane may be the turbine using steam or mercury vapor or the rocket-like blast of exploding vapor created by the combinations of yet undiscovered chemicals. The plane of the future may be a sun plane: its most notable feature will be its enormously widespread wings, the surface of which will be treated to capture the power of the sun's rays and

PREDICTION 1964 This ion-powered one-man aircraft could carry a spotter or sniper aloft.

The Power of the Future

SOONER or later we shall have to go directly to the sun for our major supply of power. This problem of the direct conversion of sunlight into power will occupy more and more of our attention as time goes on, for eventually it must be solved.—Edison Pettit, Mount Wilson Observatory.

PREDICTION

1932

Light cells may be used to produce electric energy from the sun, something already accomplished experimentally. (*See page 174.*)

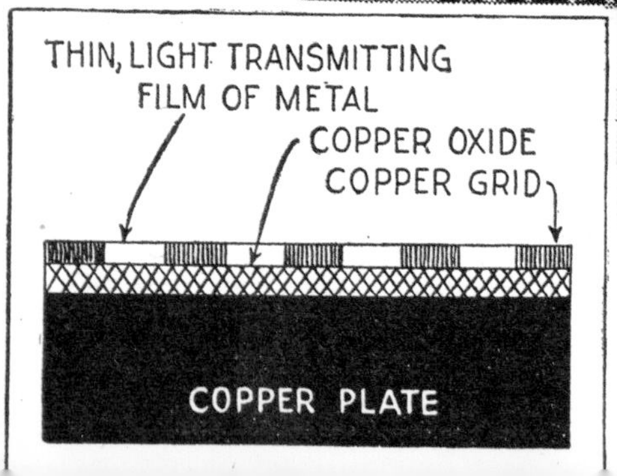

THIN, LIGHT TRANSMITTING FILM OF METAL

COPPER OXIDE

COPPER GRID

COPPER PLATE

turn this energy into enough force to lift and drive the craft. Another possibility is the magnetic plane, which would sustain its flight by establishing its own magnetic field of sufficient strength to overcome the force of gravity.

PREDICTION 1959 **Gas-turbine helicopters are looking promising.** General Electric has a navy contract for a 2,600-horsepower engine whose triple power-to-weight ratio and competitive fuel appetite promise convertiplanes and cargo helicopters of impressive range and payload. At the other extreme is Solar's tiny Titan, a one-man military helicopter engine that wraps 55 horsepower in a 50-pound package only 20 inches high. This mighty mite, to fly this year, could put wings on the foot soldier.

Recent research indicates that planes that take off vertically will be equipped with turbine engines. And an Atomic Energy Commission spokesman states that recent reactor experiments indicate that gas turbines will propel nuclear planes. Miniature gas turbines are also being used to start jet planes, operate airborne generators, and even supply extra power for taxiing.

Someday you may soar downtown in your own flying sportster—powered, of course, by a flyweight gas turbine.

THE WASTE OF THE WORLD, MATERIALIZED

PREDICTION 1907 **The currents of air that idly wander by, or harvest ruin and destruction in the form of cyclone or tornado, will in time be harnessed;** the everlasting heat of the sun made to warm the houses of men, and the mighty but now useless force of the tides put to work for the wheels of commerce.

The resident forces of electricity, now lying dormant, will lift the burden of heartbreaking toil from the shoulders of men, women and children.

The powers of nature overflow in wealth almost unheeded. Their surplus energy force tells what the future will surely bring—a better and cleaner living, the acme of the world's supremacy.

PREDICTION 1932 **The generation of power from sunlight is an old ambition.** But not until recent years has the dream come true that light can be transformed directly into electric current. The few experimental machines for generating electricity from light are inefficient. Nevertheless, discounting the undue publicity given to these devices, the generation of electric current by the direct transformation of light waves contains unknown possibilities as great as those of the radio of 30 years ago.

Will the wheels of commerce and industry one day be spun by electricity taken from the sun? Is mankind on the threshold of a revolutionary source of electrical power—one that will render obsolete the dynamo, releasing coal, oil, and gas from their bondage of servitude?

PREDICTION 1941 **From farms instead of mines and oil wells will come the coal and gasoline of the future,** Dr. Ernst Berl, research professor at the Carnegie Institute of Technology, predicts. In his laboratory, crude oil, bituminous coals, asphalts, and coke have already been produced from materials like corn, wood, algae, seaweed, leaves, and molasses. These are rich in compounds known as carbohydrates. Dr. Berl states that he can make coal or oil from carbohydrates in one to two hours. The method, he says, is "rather simple." It involves heating the carbohydrate material under pressure with limestone. He declares it cheaper than making gasoline from coal by the hydrogenation process, which requires expensive, high-pressure apparatus.

PREDICTION 1947 **Having lifted a tentative, probing finger above his head,** man is preparing to spread his arms and explore farther into the space that surrounds his earth.

Man's knowledge about cosmic rays and their relation to the energy that runs the universe may be multiplied many times by studies that are being conducted at moderate altitudes by converted B-29s and at extreme altitudes by rockets. Important new data about these powerful rays already have been obtained by means of cosmic ray telescopes placed in the warheads of V-2s by the Applied Physics Laboratory of Johns Hopkins. Showers of the rays have been recorded up to 350,000 feet.

One reason cosmic rays are the subject of widespread research today is that the energy of these particles is millions of times greater than can be produced by nuclear fission. This has very important implications in the field of atomic energy. It is entirely possible that in his upper-air research, man will find the key to a power plant that will allow him to travel even farther into space.

PREDICTION 1957 **A spaceship using a solar drive might well consist of a huge bubble of transparent polyester plastic,** suggests Krafft A. Ehricke, chief of preliminary design of Convair's astronautics division. "The bubble could be some 300 feet in diameter with a skin only one-thousandth of an inch thick," he says. "It would be slightly pressurized to give it a spherical shape. Half the inside surface would be silvered to create a hemispherical mirror that would concentrate the sun's rays on a heating element. In this element, the hydrogen would be vaporized.

One thing that isn't known is how long a large bubble can remain in good condition under the bombardment of cosmic

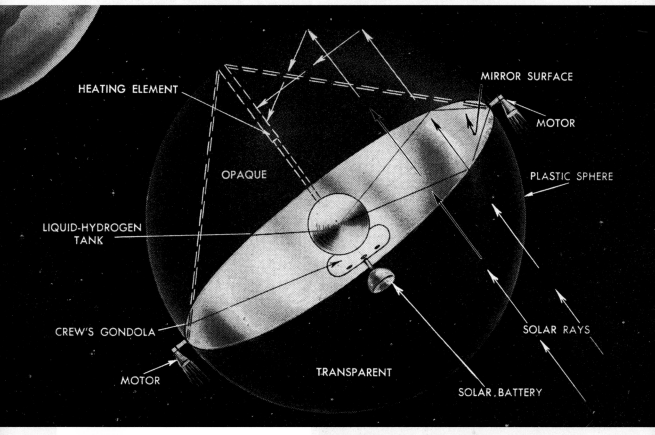

HEATING ELEMENT

MIRROR SURFACE

MOTOR

OPAQUE

PLASTIC SPHERE

LIQUID-HYDROGEN TANK

CREW'S GONDOLA

MOTOR

TRANSPARENT

SOLAR RAYS

SOLAR BATTERY

PREDICTION 1957 Solar rays heat hydrogen to power this unusual spacecraft.

dust and tiny meteors that undoubtedly exist in space. Since a round trip to Venus would take nearly a year, engineers are sure they will need to make provision for patching numerous holes in the plastic membrane during the trip. A score or more of other agencies are all doing research on portions of this problem. This includes the Air Force's Department of Space Medicine at Randolph Field, which is learning how man can live away from the earth.

MYSTERY FUELS FOR THE MISSILE AGE

PREDICTION 1938 **Looking into the future of invention, a British engineer predicts** that man may someday control gravitation—a revolutionary, inventive step that would have a greater effect on human living conditions than any previous discovery. He foresees steam power for huge aircraft, and the transmission of power through the air. Airplanes could be flown without fuel, drawing their power from beams of energy radiated along their routes.

ACETYLENE TORCH WORKS UNDER WATER

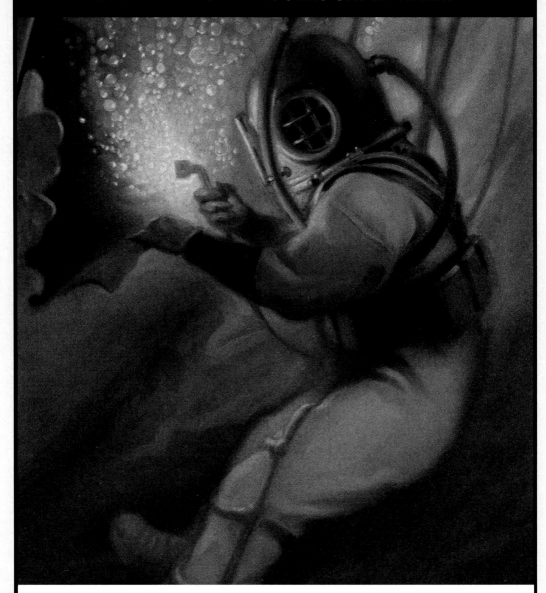

It is discovered that if a small brass cup, like the bowl of a pipe, is turned and fitted around the tip of a standard acetylene torch, turned on, and entered into the water with a diver, the flame shall remain undiminished. The pressure of the gas supply and the protection of the cup effectively force water out of its path. In this way, deep sea and emergency repairs can be made to submarines and hulls of all kinds of ships.

PREDICTION **1941** **In the near future, the beam-plane will take its power from radio stations,** just as airplanes of today are taking directional signals on beams from airport radio stations. Research engineers are already broadcasting power through the air and are lighting lamp bulbs with this unhooked energy. You may be able to get into your plane in Chicago, tune in for New York, and "click"—off you go.

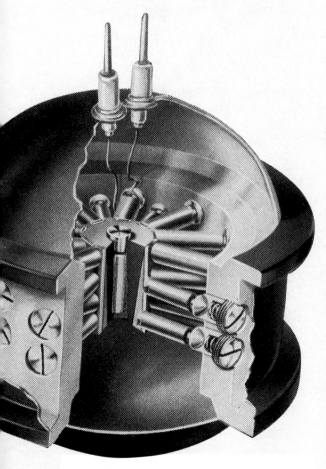

PREDICTION **1959** Radioisotopes generate heat for years without stopping, making them the perfect fuel for the thermoelectric cells of the future.

PREDICTION **1957** **Scientists are trying to contain the super-hot gases of fusion power in a "magnetic bottle."** Dr. William Phelps Allis, who heads up a fusion-research project at the Massachusetts Institute of Technology, indicates that there are "leaks" in the bottle. However, he thinks research may be developing a way to plug the leaks by superimposing another magnetic field on top of the bottle. If the method works, Dr. Allis says scientists will have learned to control fusion.

The theoretically best combination for rocket propulsion would be hydrogen as the fuel and fluorine as the oxidizer. This yields the highest heat of combustion—some 8,100 degrees—producing more thrust than other propellants. But so far, engineers haven't been able to find a way of using the combination.

PREDICTION **1963** **In a big power plant, the conversion of coal to electric watts is a three-step process:** burn fuel to create heat, make steam with the heat, then drive a turbine with the steam. The fuel cell neatly detours the heating step. By converting fuel directly into electricity, efficiency balloons up into the 80 percent region. When size and weight are figured in, the fuel cell puts out about twice the power of nickel-cadmium batteries. The comparisons are even more impressive against the ponderous lead-acid storage battery. (*Continued on page 181.*)

TO THE VACUUM OF SPACE & BEYOND

Some of tomorrow's rocket-propulsion systems may be truly fantastic. In laboratories of the National Advisory Committee for Aeronautics (NACA), scientists are poring over ion engines that they predict will propel and control future satellites in their orbits. In these tiny motors, charged bits of atoms formed in an electrical discharge are accelerated by a magnetic field, producing a high-speed jet-stream of ions at temperatures up to 20,000 degrees. NACA engineers foresee the day when that little jet will be used—in the vacuum of outer space where air-breathing engines can't operate—to move a satellite from its orbit and send it on a course to other worlds.

Operational fuel cells will tend to be used where compact lightweight power (and not costs) are critical. From now until 1965, military-space projects will surely dominate the picture. From 1965 to 1970, they should enter a limited number of mobile applications, where large vehicles are used to travel for short distances.

 PREDICTION 1963 This "air-breathing" fuel cell provides noiseless power to military field radar and radio equipment.

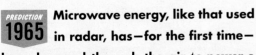 **PREDICTION 1965** **Microwave energy, like that used in radar, has—for the first time—been beamed through the air** to power a motor without wires. Demonstrating with a small tethered helicopter rotor, the Raytheon Company showed how microwaves beamed from a saucer-like transmitting antenna are converted by a rectifying antenna (a screen beaded with thousands of half-inch-long diodes), producing direct current.

Future uses of such power could be for "flying platforms" for television transmission, missile detection, aviation beacons, navigational and weather aids, and surveillance satellites.

OUR ATOM-POWERED FIGHTING FORCE

PREDICTION 1951 **Vast new reactor programs are in high gear here and abroad.** An atom-powered ship that can cruise for months without refueling is no longer pure pie in the sky. At Britain's huge Harwell Atomic Station, experimental work on a submarine powered by uranium fuel is so far along that experts are now working out figures and designs for the prototype. Our own plans for a high-speed atom-powered submarine with vastly increased range are

PREDICTION 1951 These are three possible types of nuclear-power plants for tomorrow's aircraft.

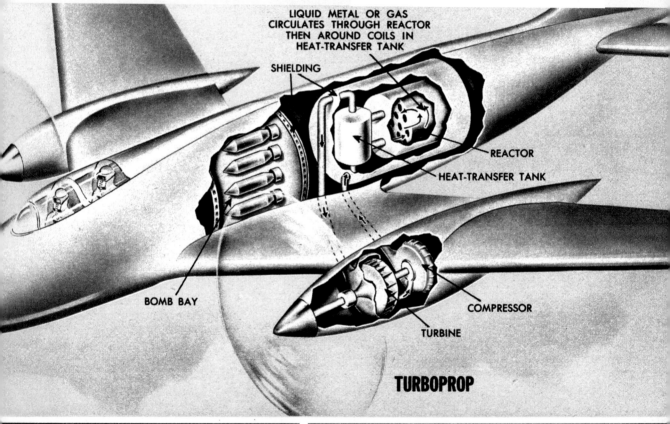

LIQUID METAL OR GAS CIRCULATES THROUGH REACTOR THEN AROUND COILS IN HEAT-TRANSFER TANK

SHIELDING

REACTOR

HEAT-TRANSFER TANK

BOMB BAY

COMPRESSOR

TURBINE

TURBOPROP

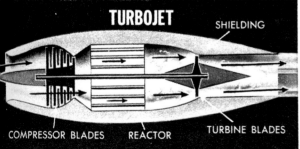

TURBOJET

SHIELDING

COMPRESSOR BLADES

REACTOR

TURBINE BLADES

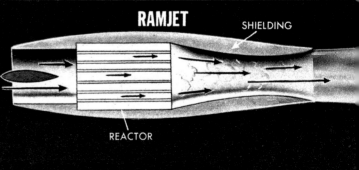

RAMJET

SHIELDING

REACTOR

complete. One navy land-based prototype of the reactor that may power the ship is already being constructed.

America's atomic submarine, according to Vice-Admiral Lockwood, will outrun, outfight, and outmaneuver any underwater or surface craft in the world. She'll have four times the horsepower of her most powerful diesel sisters. Her atomic furnace will contain plutonium—a man-contrived atomic fuel made by bombarding U-238 with fissionable uranium. Her range will be globe-girdling, since one dose of fuel will last a long, long time. Her super-streamlined hull, designed primarily for underwater cruising, will make her faster when submerged than when operating on the surface—unheard of in modern subs. She is expected to cruise down there at 25 to 30 knots and will be able to stay down for interminable periods.

To top it all, her atomic engine is expected to run so quietly that enemy electronic ears will not, in most cases, be able to hear her. Even if they do, her fantastic underwater speed will carry her safely out of danger before an enemy ship could turn around.

Even more intriguing than the atomic submarine, but also more complicated, is the idea of an airplane with a nuclear-driven power plant. It could fly nonstop around the world at supersonic speeds, ride out any bad-weather traffic stacked over an airport, and never be subject to a power failure on takeoff or landing.

PREDICTION 1956 **Rear Admiral H. G. Rickover flatly predicts that all major naval ships** built after 1960 will be powered by reactors. And it now appears that the first nuclear-powered aircraft carrier will be finished sometime in 1961. According to Admiral Arleigh Burke, this ship will be about as big as the U.S.S. *Forrestal,* though quite different in appearance, as it will have no stacks and will boast two separate island superstructures. The goal is to rebuild the navy from the keel up into a high-speed, atomic-powered striking force.

PREDICTION 1957 **Recently we've been hearing about nuclear-powered planes** that will fly eighty times around the world without refueling, carry hordes of passengers to remote places at supersonic speeds, and pull trains of gliders all over the skies. Some of these guesses are plausible, says Dr. Lyle B. Borst, chairman of the physics department at New York University, but "the first problem will be to get it off the ground. Ten years is a realistic estimate of the time it might take to put the first atom-powered plane in the air. That plane probably will be a long-range bomber."

Regarding the design of such an aircraft, Dr. Borst notes that the crew will want to be as far from the reactor as they can get, and crew quarters would have to be as small as possible to minimize the weight of the crew shield. "One thinks sometimes about what is practically a

WHALE-SHAPED SUB *ZIPS THROUGH THE WATER*

This whale-shaped nuclear attack sub, still on the drawing boards, will "fly" at phenomenal speeds under the sea the way a plane flies through the air, pilot and co-pilot strapped to bucket seats while crew members grab for leather loops like subway straphangers as the weird craft executes high-speed turns at a 30-degree bank.

flying arrow, with the reactor near the tail feathers and the crew near the arrow head. One would probably not want to use a crew of more than three, and they would be very confined; they would not have walkways, galleys, bunks, or anything like that. We may be going back to the very old planes, where you had tandem cockpits." That could get uncomfortable on the plane's predicted 18-hour flights.

Mr. Frederick K. Teichmann, assistant dean of NYU's College of Engineering, says the first atomic plane may be a huge seaplane. "It might be compared to a flying aircraft carrier with a flat deck for the smaller airplanes to land," he says. "It has disappearing elevators, to carry planes up from and down to the storage hold."

Some usages of the atom-powered airplanes of the future include search and patrol missions in which the ability to stay aloft for indefinite periods of time is important, and special missions of plane groups that must rendezvous but must be capable of meeting delayed elements of the rendezvous.

Servicing an atomic plane will be difficult. Dr. Borst, noting the difficulty of refueling a reactor that is highly radio-active, suggests replacing the entire reactor after every 14,000-mile trip. Another option is to refuel the reactor via remote-controlled robot.

WE'RE GOING TO WORK MIRACLES

PREDICTION 1945 **Peaceful harnessing of the atomic bomb will have been achieved within five years,** and within ten years it will be the useful servant of man in a score of different ways. Here, controlled nuclear explosions will open a new harbor in the Alaskan ice.

There is speculation about the possibility of some weather control by atomic forces. The mayor of a Florida city asked that a bomb be exploded in the midst of a hurricane to see if it might scatter or check it. That raises the question whether something akin to a vast tidal wave might be started whose destructiveness would be still greater.

A tremendous iceberg sank the *Titanic*, the luxurious liner that was the pride of all the seas in its day, back in 1912. Even today icebergs are a menace to navigation, and their presence must be taken into account in charting the courses of vessels. Atom bombs, or well-placed atomic explosive charges, offer the possibility of clearing the oceans of these floating dangers. Broken into icy slivers, they might dissolve in the warmer water and disappear.

Explosions that level cities can also lay waste many a granite "hell gate" where ships totter into a watery grave. And as we may clear old channels, we may well make new ones. With atomic power controlled, as it will be just as other natural forces have been harnessed, a new Panama Canal could be possible in weeks instead of years.

One may see another variant of the use of atomic energy in earth removal. That is in strip-mining. In many coal and iron ore regions, the veins are only a few feet, maybe 15 or 20, below the surface. Stripping off the top dirt is a tedious job. Atomic explosives can be visualized as performing this task in minutes.

Time will be required, of course, to refine atomic power to the point where it can be used for precision jobs. But that will come, sooner perhaps than many of us think. No one can chart the future, but evidence is at hand that the greatest magic carpet of all the ages is being unrolled. It remains for man to use it for his own good rather than his ruin. But we need not fear. In the long run, man usually chooses the thing that will keep him going and improve his lot—at least an atomic trifle!

PREDICTION 1945 Controlled nuclear explosions will open a harbor in the Alaskan ice.

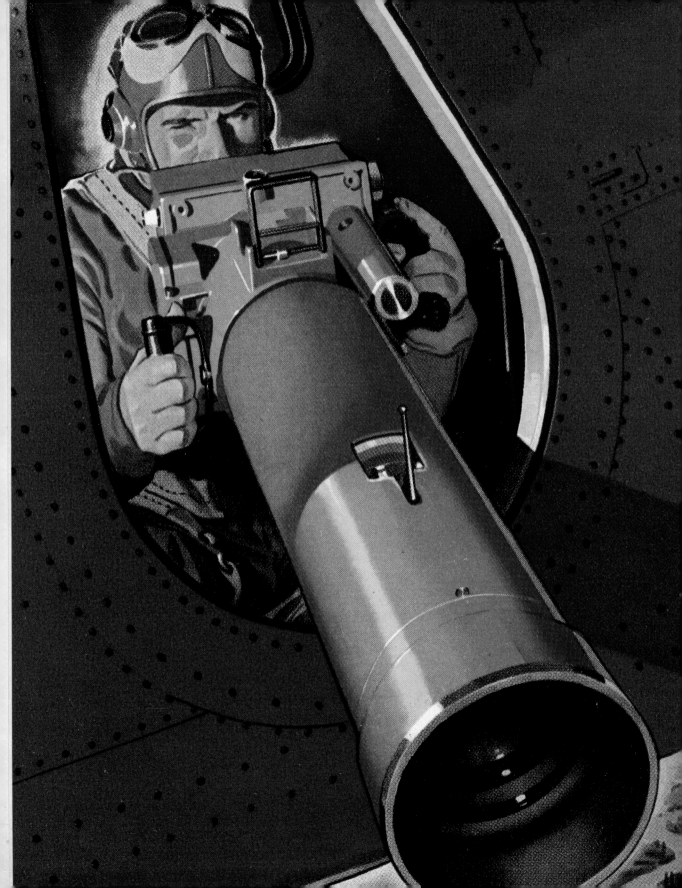

GENERAL INDEX

PAGE 36

1925 **EXPERIMENTAL DEATH RAYS** These powerful beams may someday be used to destroy airplanes and other machines of war.

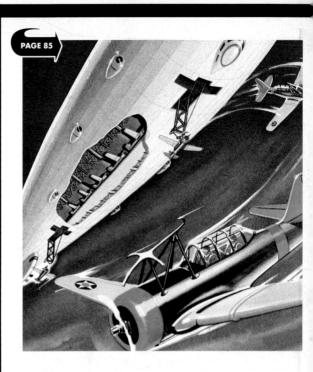

PAGE 85

1942 **DIRIGIBLE "MOTHER SHIP"** Planes will soon be launched and retrieved by airships.

PAGE 67

1928 **SUPER-SENSITIVE SOUND COLLECTORS** These are the "ears" of self-aiming anti-aircraft guns that track airplanes by sound.

PAGE 92

1932 **NEWEST AIR MENACE** Flying tanks are expected to take off through mud or bumpy ground.